The Dynasts by Thomas Hardy

AN EPIC-DRAMA OF THE WAR WITH NAPOLEON, IN THREE PARTS

PART SECOND

The Time covered by the Action being about ten Years

"And I heard sounds of insult, shame, and wrong,
And trumpets blown for wars."

Many giants of Literature originate from the shores of these emerald isles; Shakespeare, Dickens, Chaucer, The Brontes and Austen to which most people would willingly add the name Thomas Hardy.

'Far From The Madding Crowd',' Tess Of The D'Urbervilles', 'The Mayor Of Casterbridge' are but three of his literary masterpieces.

In fact, Hardy himself thought he was a poet who wrote novels purely for the money. Indeed his poems were not published until he was in his fifties after his major novels were published and his reputation set. His novels of course continue to influence and mentor our thoughts.

Each is a journey through a mind that creates characters, landscapes and narratives that reveal themselves in rich and textured detail as few other writers are able to do.

Index of Contents

CHARACTERS

I. PHANTOM INTELLIGENCES
THE ANCIENT SPIRIT OF THE YEARS/CHORUS OF THE YEARS.

THE SPIRIT OF THE PITIES/CHORUS OF THE PITIES.
SPIRITS SINISTER AND IRONIC/CHORUSES OF SINISTER AND IRONIC SPIRITS.
THE SPIRIT OF RUMOUR/CHORUS OF RUMOURS.
THE SHADE OF THE EARTH.

SPIRIT-MESSENGERS.
RECORDING ANGELS.

II. PERSONS [The names in lower case are mute figures.]
MEN
GEORGE THE THIRD.
THE PRINCE OF WALES, afterwards PRINCE REGENT.
The Royal Dukes.
FOX.
PERCEVAL.
CASTLEREAGH.
AN UNDER-SECRETARY OF STATE.
SHERIDAN.
TWO YOUNG LORDS.
Lords Yarmouth and Keith.
ANOTHER LORD.
Other Peers, Ambassadors, Ministers, ex-Ministers, Members of
Parliament, and Persons of Quality and Office.
....
Sir Arthur Wellesley, afterwards Lord Wellington.
SIR JOHN MOORE.
SIR JOHN HOPE.
Sir David Baird.
General Beresford.
COLONEL ANDERSON.
COLONEL GRAHAM.
MAJOR COLBORNE, principal Aide-de-Camp to MOORE.
CAPTAIN HARDINGE.
Paget, Fraser, Hill, Napier.
A CAPTAIN OF HUSSARS AND OTHERS.
Other English Generals, Colonels, Aides, Couriers, and Military
Officers.
TWO SPIES.
TWO ARMY SURGEONS.
AN ARMY CHAPLAIN.
A SERGEANT OF THE FORTY-THIRD.
TWO SOLDIERS OF THE NINTH.
English Forces.
DESERTERS AND STRAGGLERS.
....
DR. WILLIS.
SIR HENRY HALFORD.
DR. HEBERDEN.
DR. BAILLIE.
THE KING'S APOTHECARY.
A GENTLEMAN.
TWO ATTENDANTS ON THE KING.
....

MEMBERS OF A LONDON CLUB.
AN ENGLISHMAN IN VIENNA.
TROTTER, SECRETARY TO FOX.
MR. BAGOT.
MR. FORTH, MASTER OF CEREMONIES.
SERVANTS.
A Beau, A Constable, etc.
....
NAPOLEON BONAPARTE.
Joseph Bonaparte.
Louis and Jerome Bonaparte, and other Members of Napoleon's Family.
CAMBACERES, ARCH-CHANCELLOR.
TALLEYRAND.
PRESIDENT OF THE SENATE.
Caulaincourt.
Lebrun, Duroc, Prince of Neufchatel, Grand-Duke of Berg.
Eugene de Beauharnais.
CHAMPAGNY, FOREIGN MINISTER
DE BAUSSET, CHAMBERLAIN.
MURAT.
SOULT.
MASSENA.
BERTHIER.
JUNOT.
FOY.
LOISON.
Ney, Lannes, and other French Marshals, general and regimental
Officers, Aides, and Couriers.
TWO FRENCH SUBALTERNS.
ANOTHER FRENCH OFFICER.
French Forces.
....
Grand Marshal, Grand Almoners, Heralds, and other Officials at
Napoleon's marriage.
ABBE DE PRADT, CHAPEL-MASTER.
Corvisart, First Physician to Marie Louis.
BOURDIER, SECOND PHYSICIAN to Marie Louise.
DUBOIS, ACCOUCHEUR to Marie Louise.
Maskers at a Ball.
TWO SERVANTS AT THE TUILERIES.
A PARISIAN CROWD.
GUILLET DE GEVRILLIERE, A CONSPIRATOR.
Louis XVIII. of France.
French Princes in England.
....
THE KING OF PRUSSIA.
Prince Henry of Prussia.
Prince Royal of Bavaria.

PRINCE HOHENLOHE.
Generals Ruchel, Tauenzien, and Attendant Officers.
Prussian Forces.
PRUSSIAN STRAGGLERS.
BERLIN CITIZENS.
....
CARLOS IV., KING OF SPAIN.
FERNANDO, PRINCE OF ASTURIAS, Son to the King.
GODOY, "PRINCE OF PEACE," Lover of the Queen.
COUNT OF MONTIJO.
VISCOUNT MATEROSA, Spanish Deputy.
DON DIEGO DE LA VEGA, Spanish Deputy.
Godoy's Guards and other Soldiery.
SPANISH CITIZENS.
A SERVANT TO GODOY.
Spanish Forces.
Camp-Followers.
....
FRANCIS, EMPEROR OF AUSTRIA.
METTERNICH.
ANOTHER AUSTRIAN MINISTER.
SCHWARZENBERG.
D'AUDENARDE, AN EQUERRY.
AUSTRIAN OFFICERS.
AIDES-DE-CAMP.
Austrian Forces.
Couriers and Secretaries.
VIENNESE CITIZENS.
....
THE EMPEROR ALEXANDER.
The Grand-Duke Constantine.
Prince Labanoff.
Count Lieven.
Generals Bennigsen, Ouwaroff, and others.
Officers in attendance on Alexander.

WOMEN
CAROLINE, PRINCESS OF WALES.
DUCHESS OF YORK.
DUCHESS OF RUTLAND.
MARCHIONESS OF SALISBURY.
MARCHIONESS OF HERTFORD.
Other Peeresses.
MRS. FITZHERBERT.
Ambassadors' Wives, Wives of Minister and Members of Parliament, and other Ladies of Note.
....
THE EMPRESS JOSEPHINE.
HORTENSE, QUEEN OF HOLLAND.

The Mother of Napoleon.
Princess Pauline, and others of Napoleon's Family.
DUCHESS OF MONTEBELLO.
MADAME DE MONTESQUIOU.
MADAME BLAISE, NURSE TO MARIE LOUIS.
Wives of French Ministers, and of other Officials.
Other Ladies of the French Court.
DUCHESS OF ANGOULEME.

....

LOUISA, QUEEN OF PRUSSIA.
The Countess Voss, Lady-in-Waiting.
BERLIN LADIES.

....

MARIA LUISA, QUEEN OF SPAIN.
THEREZA OF BOURBON, WIFE OF GODOY.
DONA JOSEFA TUDO, MISTRESS OF GODOY.
Lady-in-Waiting to the Queen.
A Servant.

....

M. LOUISA BEATRIX, EMPRESS OF AUSTRIA.
THE ARCHDUCHESS MARIE LOUISA, afterwards the EMPRESS MARIE LOUISE.
MADAME METTERNICH.
LADIES OF THE AUSTRIAN COURT.

....

THE EMPRESS-MOTHER OF RUSSIA.
GRAND-DUCHESS ANNE OF RUSSIA.

ACT FIRST

SCENE I

LONDON. FOX'S LODGINGS, ARLINGTON STREET

[FOX, the Foreign Secretary in the new Ministry of All-the-Talents, sits at a table writing. He is a stout, swarthy man, with shaggy eyebrows, and his breathing is somewhat obstructed. His clothes look as though they had been slept in. TROTTER, his private secretary, is writing at another table near. A servant enters.]

SERVANT
Another stranger presses to see you, sir.

FOX [without raising his eyes]
Oh, another. What's he like?

SERVANT

A foreigner, sir; though not so out-at-elbows as might be thought from the denomination. He says he's from Gravesend, having lately left Paris, and that you sent him a passport. He comes with a police-officer.

FOX
Ah, to be sure. I remember. Bring him in, and tell the officer to wait outside. [Servant goes out.] Trotter, will you leave us for a few minutes? But be within hail.

[The secretary retires, and the servant shows in a man who calls himself GUILLET DE GEVRILLIERE—a tall, thin figure of thirty, with restless eyes. The door being shut behind him, he is left alone with the minister. FOX points to a seat, leans back, and surveys his visitor.]

GEVRILLIERE
Thanks to you, sir, for this high privilege
Of hailing England, and of entering here.
Without a fore-extended confidence
Like this of yours, my plans would not have sped. [A Pause.]
Europe, alas! sir, has her waiting foot
Upon the sill of further slaughter-scenes!

FOX
I fear it is so!—In your lines you wrote,
I think, that you are a true Frenchman born?

GEVRILLIERE
I did, sir.

FOX
How contrived you, then, to cross?

GEVRILLIERE
It was from Embden that I shipped for Gravesend,
In a small sailer called the "Toby," sir,
Masked under Prussian colours. Embden I reached
On foot, on horseback, and by sundry shifts,
From Paris over Holland, secretly.

FOX
And you are stored with tidings of much pith,
Whose tenour would be priceless to the state?

GEVRILLIERE
I am. It is, in brief, no more nor less
Than means to mitigate and even end
These welfare-wasting wars; ay, usher in
A painless spell of peace.

FOX

Prithee speak on.
No statesman can desire it more than I.

GEVRILLIERE [looking to see that the door is shut]
No nation, sir, can live its natural life,
Or think its thoughts in these days unassailed,
No crown-capt head enjoy tranquillity.
The fount of such high spring-tide of disorder,
Fevered disquietude, and forceful death,
Is One,—a single man. He—need I name?—
The ruler is of France.

FOX
Well, in the past
I fear that it has liked so. But we see
Good reason still to hope that broadening views,
Politer wisdom now is helping him
To saner guidance of his arrogant car.

GEVRILLIERE
The generous hope will never be fulfilled!
Ceasing to bluff, then ceases he to be.
None sees that written largelier than himself.

FOX
Then what may be the valued revelation
That you can unlock in such circumstance?
Sir, I incline to spell you as a spy,
And not the honest help for honest men
You gave you out to be!

GEVRILLIERE
I beg, sir,
To spare me that suspicion. Never a thought
Could be more groundless. Solemnly I vow
That notwithstanding what his signals show
The Emperor of France is as I say.—
Yet bring I good assurance, and declare
A medicine for all bruised Europe's sores!

FOX [impatiently]
Well, parley to the point, for I confess
No new negotiation do I note
That you can open up to work such cure.

GEVRILLIERE
The sovereign remedy for an ill effect
Is the extinction of its evil cause.

Safely and surely how to compass this
I have the weighty honour to disclose,
Certain immunities being guaranteed
By those your power can influence, and yourself.

FOX [astonished]
Assassination?

GEVRILLIERE
I care not for names!
A deed's true name is as its purpose is.
The lexicon of Liberty and Peace
Defines not this deed as assassination;
Though maybe it is writ so in the tongue
Of courts and universal tyranny.

FOX
Why brought you this proposal here to me?

GEVRILLIERE
My knowledge of your love of things humane,
Things free, things fair, of truth, of tolerance,
Right, justice, national felicity,
Prompted belief and hope in such a man!—
The matter is by now well forwarded,
A house at Plassy hired as pivot-point
From which the sanct intention can be worked,
And soon made certain. To our good allies
No risk attaches; merely to ourselves.
FOX [touching a private bell]

Sir, your unconscienced hardihood confounds me.
And your mind's measure of my character
Insults it sorely. By your late-sent lines
Of specious import, by your bland address,
I have been led to prattle hopefully
With a cut-throat confessed!

[The head constable and the secretary enter at the same moment.]

Ere worse befall,
Sir, up and get you gone most dexterously!
Conduct this man: lose never sight of him [to the officer]
Till haled aboard some anchor-weighing craft
Bound to remotest coasts from us and France.

GEVRILLIERE [unmoved]
How you may handle me concerns me little.

The project will as roundly ripe itself
Without as with me. Trusty souls remain,
Though my far bones bleach white on austral shores!—
I thank you for the audience. Long ere this
I might have reft your life! Ay, notice here—

[He produces a dagger; which is snatched from him.]

They need not have done that! Even had you risen
To wrestle with, insult, strike, pinion me,
It would have lain unused. In hands like mine
And my allies', the man of peace is safe,
Treat as he may our corporal tenement
In his misreading of a moral code.

[Exeunt GEVRILLIERE and the constable.]

FOX
Trotter, indeed you well may stare at me!
I look warm, eh?—and I am windless, too;
I have sufficient reason to be so.
That dignified and pensive gentleman
Was a bold bravo, waiting for his chance.
He sketched a scheme for murdering Bonaparte,
Either—as in my haste I understood—
By shooting from a window as he passed,
Or by some other wry and stealthy means
That haunt sad brains which brood on despotism,
But lack the tools to justly cope therewith!...
On later thoughts I feel not fully sure
If, in my ferment, I did right in this.
No; hail at once the man in charge of him,
And give the word that he is to be detained.

[The secretary goes out. FOX walks to the window in deep reflection till the secretary returns.]

SECRETARY
I was in time, sir. He has been detained.

FOX
Now what does strict state-honour ask of me?—
No less than that I bare this poppling plot
To the French ruler and our fiercest foe!—
Maybe 'twas but a hoax to pocket pay;
And yet it can mean more...
The man's indifference to his own vague doom
Beamed out as one exalted trait in him,
And showed the altitude of his rash dream!—

Well, now I'll get me on to Downing Street,
There to draw up a note to Talleyrand
Retailing him the facts.—What signature
Subscribed this desperate fellow when he wrote?

SECRETARY
"Guillet de la Gevrilliere." Here it stands.

FOX
Doubtless it was a false one. Come along. [Looking out the window.]
Ah—here's Sir Francis Vincent: he'll go with us.
Ugh, what a twinge! Time signals that he draws
Towards the twelfth stroke of my working-day!
I fear old England soon must voice her speech
With Europe through another mouth than mine!

SECRETARY
I trust not, sir. Though you should rest awhile.
The very servants half are invalid
From the unceasing labours of your post,
And these cloaked visitors of every clime
That market on your magnanimity
To gain an audience morning, night, and noon,
Leaving you no respite.

FOX
'Tis true; 'tis true.—
How I shall love my summer holiday
At pleasant Saint-Ann's Hill!

[He leans on the secretary's arm, and they go out.]

SCENE II

THE ROUTE BETWEEN LONDON AND PARIS

[A view now nocturnal, now diurnal, from on high over the Straits of Dover, and stretching from city to city. By night Paris and London seem each as a little swarm of lights surrounded by a halo; by day as a confused glitter of white and grey. The Channel between them is as a mirror reflecting the sky, brightly or faintly, as the hour may be.]

SPIRIT OF THE PITIES
What mean these couriers shooting shuttlewise
To Paris and to London, turn and turn?

RUMOURS [chanting in antiphons]

I
The aforesaid tidings fro the minister, spokesman in England's cause to states afar,

II
Traverse the waters borne by one of such; and thereto Bonaparte's responses are:

I
"The principles of honour and of truth which ever actuate the sender's mind

II
"Herein are written largely! Take our thanks: we read that this conjuncture undesigned

I
"Unfolds felicitous means of showing you that still our eyes are set, as yours, on peace,

II
"To which great end the Treaty of Amiens must be the ground-work of our amities."

I
From London then: "The path to amity the King of England studies to pursue;

II
"With Russia hand in hand he is yours to close the long convulsions thrilling Europe through."

I
Still fare the shadowy missioners across, by Dover-road and Calais Channel-track,

II
From Thames-side towers to Paris palace-gates; from Paris leisurely to London back.

I
Till thus speaks France: "Much grief it gives us that, being pledged to treat, one Emperor with one King,

II
"You yet have struck a jarring counternote and tone that keys not with such promising.

I
"In these last word, then, of this pregnant parle; I trust I may persuade your Excellency

II
"That in no circumstance, on no pretence, a party to our pact can Russia be."

SPIRIT SINISTER
Fortunately for the manufacture of corpses by machinery Napoleon sticks to this veto, and so wards off the awkward catastrophe of a general peace descending upon Europe. Now England.

RUMOURS [continuing]
I

Thereon speeds down through Kent and Picardy, evenly as some southing sky-bird's shade:

II
"We gather not from your Imperial lines a reason why our words should be reweighed.

I
"We hold Russia not as our ally that is to be: she stands fully-plighted so;

II
"Thus trembles peace upon this balance-point: will you that Russia be let in or no?"

I
Then France rolls out rough words across the strait: "To treat with you confederate with the Tsar,

II
"Presumes us sunk in sloughs of shamefulness from which we yet stand gloriously afar!

I
"The English army must be Flanders-fed, and entering Picardy with pompous prance,

II
"To warrant such! Enough. Our comfort is, the crime of further strife lies not with France."

SPIRIT OF THE PITIES
Alas! what prayer will save the struggling lands,
Whose lives are ninepins to these bowling hands?

CHORUS OF RUMOURS
France secretly with—Russia plights her troth!
Britain, that lonely isle, is slurred by both.

SPIRIT SINISTER
It is as neat as an uncovered check at chess! You may now mark Fox's blank countenance at finding himself thus rewarded for the good turn done to Bonaparte, and at the extraordinary conduct of his chilly friend the Muscovite.

SPIRIT OF THE PITIES
His hand so trembles it can scarce retain
The quill wherewith he lets Lord Yarmouth know
Reserve is no more needed!

SPIRIT IRONIC
Now enters another character of this remarkable little piece—Lord
Lauderdale—and again the messengers fly!

SPIRIT OF THE PITIES
But what strange figure, pale and noiseless, comes,
By us perceived, unrecognized by those,

Into the very closet and retreat
Of England's Minister?

SPIRIT OF THE YEARS
The Tipstaff he
Of the Will, the Many-masked, my good friend Death.—
The statesman's feeble form you may perceive
Now hustled into the Invisible,
And the unfinished game of Dynasties
Left to proceed without him!

SPIRIT OF THE PITIES
Here, then, ends
My hope for Europe's reason-wrought repose!
He was the friend of peace—did his great best
To shed her balms upon humanity;
And now he's gone! No substitute remains.

SPIRIT IRONIC
Ay; the remainder of the episode is frankly farcical. Negotiations are again affected; but finally you
discern Lauderdale applying for passports; and the English Parliament declares to the nation that peace
with France cannot be made.

RUMOURS [concluding]
I
The smouldering dudgeon of the Prussian king, meanwhile, upon the horizon's rim afar

II
Bursts into running flame, that all his signs of friendliness were met by moves for war.

I
Attend and hear, for hear ye faintly may, his manifesto made at Erfurt town,

II
That to arms only dares he now confide the safety and the honour of his crown!

SPIRIT OF THE YEARS
Draw down the curtain, then, and overscreen
This too-protracted verbal fencing-scene;
And let us turn to clanging foot and horse,
Ordnance, and all the enginry of Force!

[Clouds close over the perspective.]

SCENE III

[It is afternoon, and the thoroughfares are crowded with citizens in an excited and anxious mood. A central path is left open for some expected arrival.

There enters on horseback a fair woman, whose rich brown curls stream flutteringly in the breeze, and whose long blue habit flaps against the flank of her curvetting white mare. She is the renowned LOUISA, QUEEN OF PRUSSIA, riding at the head of a regiment of hussars and wearing their uniform. As she prances along the thronging citizens acclaim her enthusiastically.]

SPIRIT OF THE PITIES
Who is this fragile fair, in fighting trim?

SPIRIT OF THE YEARS
She is the pride of Prussia, whose resolve
Gives ballast to the purpose of her spouse,
And holds him to what men call governing.

SPIRIT OF THE PITIES
Queens have engaged in war; but war's loud trade
Rings with a roar unnatural, fitful, forced,
Practised by woman's hands!

SPIRIT OF THE YEARS
Of her view
The enterprise is that of scores of men,
The strength but half-a-ones.

SPIRIT OF THE PITIES
Would fate had ruled
The valour had been his, hers but the charm!

SPIRIT OF RUMOUR
But he has nothing on't, and she has all.
The shameless satires of the bulletins
dispatched to Paris, thence the wide world through,
Disturb the dreams of her by those who love her,
And thus her brave adventurers for the realm
Have blurred her picture, soiled her gentleness,
And wrought her credit harm.

FIRST CITIZEN [vociferously]
Yes, by God: send and ultimatum to Paris, by God; that's what we'll do, by God. The Confederation of the Rhine was the evil thought of an evil man bent on ruining us!

SECOND CITIZEN
This country double-faced and double-tongued,
This France, or rather say, indeed, this Man—

[Peoples are honest dealers in the mass]—
This man, to sign a stealthy scroll with Russia
That shuts us off from all indemnities,
While swearing faithful friendship with our King,
And, still professing our safe wardenry,
To fatten other kingdoms at our cost,
Insults us grossly, and makes Europe clang
With echoes of our wrongs. The little states
Of this antique and homely German land
Are severed from their blood-allies and kin—
Hereto of one tradition, interest, hope—
In calling lord this rank adventurer,
Who'll thrust them as a sword against ourselves.—
Surely Great Frederick sweats within his tomb!

THIRD CITIZEN
Well, we awake, though we have slumbered long,
And She is sent by Heaven to kindle us.

[The QUEEN approaches to pass back again with her suite. The vociferous applause is repeated. They regard her as she nears.]

To cry her Amazon, a blusterer,
A brazen comrade of the bold dragoons
Whose uniform she dons! Her, whose each act
Shows but a mettled modest woman's zeal,
Without a hazard of her dignity
Or moment's sacrifice of seemliness,
To fend off ill from home!

FOURTH CITIZEN [entering]
The tidings fly that Russian Alexander
Declines with emphasis to ratify
The pact of his ambassador with France,
And that the offer made the English King
To compensate the latter at our cost
Has not been taken.

THIRD CITIZEN
And it never will be!
Thus evil does not always flourish, faith.
Throw down the gage while god is fair to us;
He may be foul anon!

[A pause.]

FIFTH CITIZEN [entering]

Our ambassador Lucchesini is already leaving Paris. He could stand the Emperor no longer, so the Emperor takes his place, has decided to order his snuff by the ounce and his candles by the pound, lest he should not be there long enough to use more.

[The QUEEN goes by, and they gaze at here and at the escort of soldiers.]

Haven't we soldiers? Haven't we the Duke of Brunswick to command 'em? Haven't we provisions, hey? Haven't we fortresses and an Elbe, to bar the bounce of an invader?

[The cavalcade passes out of sight and the crowd draws off.]

FIRST CITIZEN
By God, I must to beer and 'bacco, to soften my rage!

[Exeunt citizens.]

SPIRIT OF THE YEARS
So doth the Will objectify Itself
In likeness of a sturdy people's wrath,
Which takes no count of the new trends of time,
Trusting ebbed glory in a present need.—
What if their strength should equal not their fire,
And their devotion dull their vigilance?—
Uncertainly, by fits, the Will doth work
In Brunswick's blood, their chief, as in themselves;
It ramifies in streams that intermit
And make their movement vague, old-fashioned, slow
To foil the modern methods counterposed!

[Evening descends on the city, and it grows dusk. The soldiers being dismissed from duty, some young officers in a frolic of defiance halt, draw their swords and whet them on the steps of the FRENCH AMBASSADOR'S residence as they pass. The noise of whetting is audible through the street.]

CHORUS OF THE PITIES [aerial music]
The soul of a nation distrest
Is aflame,
And heaving with eager unrest
In its aim
To assert its old prowess, and stouten its chronicled fame!

SEMICHORUS I
It boils in a boisterous thrill
Through the mart,
Unconscious well-nigh as the Will
Of its part:
Would it wholly might be so, and feel not the forthcoming smart!

SEMICHORUS II

In conclaves no voice of reflection
Is heard,
King, Councillors, grudge circumspection
A word,
And victory is visioned, and seemings as facts are averred.

CHORUS
Yea, the soul of a nation distrest
Is aflame,
And heaving with eager unrest
In its aim
At supreme desperations to blazon the national name!

[Midnight strikes, lights are extinguished one by one, and the scene disappears.]

SCENE IV

THE FIELD OF JENA

[Day has just dawned through a grey October haze. The French, with their backs to the nebulous light, loom out and show themselves to be already under arms; LANNES holding the centre, NEY the right, SOULT the extreme right, and AUGEREAU the left. The Imperial Guard and MURAT'S cavalry are drawn up on the Landgrafenberg, behind the centre of the French position. In a valley stretching along to the rear of this height flows northward towards the Elbe the little river Saale, on which the town of Jena stands.

On the irregular plateaux in front of the French lines, and almost close to the latter, are the Prussians un TAUENZIEN; and away on their right rear towards Weimar the bulk of the army under PRINCE HOHENLOHE. The DUKE OF BRUNSWICK [father of the Princess of Wales] is twelve miles off with his force at Auerstadt, in the valley of the Ilm.

Enter NAPOLEON, and men bearing torches who escort him. He moves along the front of his troops, and is lost to view behind the mist and surrounding objects. But his voice is audible.]

NAPOLEON
Keep you good guard against their cavalry,
In past repute the formidablest known,
And such it may be now; so asks our heed.
Receive it, then, in square, unflinchingly.—
Remember, men, last year you captured Ulm,
So make no doubt that you will vanquish these!

SOLDIERS
Long live the Emperor! Advance, advance!

DUMB SHOW

Almost immediately glimpses reveal that LANNES' corps is moving forward, and amid an unbroken clatter of firelocks spreads out further and wider upon the stretch of country in front of the Landgrafenberg. The Prussians, surprised at discerning in the fog such masses of the enemy close at hand, recede towards the Ilm.

From PRINCE HOHENLOHE, who is with the body of the Prussians on the Weimar road to the south, comes perspiring the bulk of the infantry to rally the retreating regiments of TAUENZIEN, and he hastens up himself with the cavalry and artillery. The action is renewed between him and NEY as the clocks of Jena strike ten.

But AUGEREAU is seen coming to Ney's assistance on one flank of the Prussians, SOULT bearing down on the other, while NAPOLEON on the Landgrafenberg orders the Imperial Guard to advance. The doomed Prussians are driven back, this time more decisively, falling in great numbers and losing many as prisoners as they reel down the sloping land towards the banks of the Ilm behind them. GENERAL RUCHEL, in a last despairing effort to rally, faces the French onset in person and alone. He receives a bullet through the chest and falls dead.

The crisis of the struggle is reached, though the battle is not over. NAPOLEON, discerning from the Landgrafenberg that the decisive moment has come, directs MURAT to sweep forward with all his cavalry. It engages the shattered Prussians, surrounds them, and cuts them down by thousands.

From behind the horizon, a dozen miles off, between the din of guns in the visible battle, there can be heard an ominous roar, as of a second invisible battle in progress there. Generals and other officers look at each other and hazard conjectures between whiles, the French with exultation, the Prussians gloomily.

HOHENLOHE
That means the Duke of Brunswick, I conceive,
Impacting on the enemy's further force
Led by, they say, Davout and Bernadotte.
God grant his star less lurid rays then ours,
Or this too pregnant, hoarsely-groaning day
Shall, ere its loud delivery be done,
Have twinned disasters to the fatherland
That fifty years will fail to sepulchre!

Enter a straggler on horseback.

STRAGGLER
Prince, I have circuited by Auerstadt,
And bring ye dazzling tidings of the fight,
Which, if report by those who saw't be true,
Has raged thereat from clammy day-dawn on,
And left us victors!

HOHENLOHE
Thitherward go I,
And patch the mischief wrought upon us here!

Enter a second and then a third straggler.

Well, wet-faced men, whence come ye? What d'ye bring?

STRAGGLER II
Your Highness, I rode straight from Hassenhausen,
Across the stream of battle as it boiled
Betwixt that village and the banks of Saale,
And such the turmoil that no man could speak
On what the issue was!

HOHENLOHE [To Straggler III]
Can you add aught?

STRAGGLER III
Nothing that's clear, your Highness.

HOHENLOHE
Man, your mien
Is that of one who knows, but will not say.
Detain him here.

STRAGGLER III
The blackness of my news,
Your Highness, darks my sense!... I saw this much:
His charging grenadiers, received in the face
A grape-shot stroke that gouged out half of it,
Proclaiming then and there his life fordone.

HOHENLOHE
Fallen? Brunswick! Reed in council, rock in fire...
Ah, this he looked for. Many a time of late
Has he, by some strange gift of foreknowing,
Declared his fate was hovering in such wise!

STRAGGLER III
His aged form being borne beyond the strife,
The gallant Moellendorf, in flushed despair,
Swore he would not survive; and, pressing on,
He, too, was slaughtered. Patriotic rage
Brimmed marshals' breasts and men's. The King himself
Fought like the commonest. But nothing served.
His horse is slain; his own doom yet unknown.
Prince William, too, is wounded. Brave Schmettau
Is broke; himself disabled. All give way,
And regiments crash like trees at felling-time!

HOHENLOHE
No more. We match it here. The yielding lines
Still sweep us backward. Backward we must go!

[Exeunt HOHENLOHE, Staff, stragglers, etc.]

The Prussian retreat from Jena quickens to a rout, many thousands taken prisoners by MURAT, who
pursues them to Weimar, where the inhabitants fly shrieking through the streets.

The October day closes in to evening. By this time the troops retiring with the King of Prussia from the
second battlefield of Auerstadt have intersected RUCHEL'S and HOHENLOHE'S flying battalions from
Jena. The crossing streams of fugitives strike panic into each other, and the tumult increases with the
thickening darkness till night renders the scene invisible, and nothing remains but a confused
diminishing noise, and fitful lights here and there.

SCENE V

BERLIN. A ROOM OVERLOOKING A PUBLIC PLACE

[A fluttering group of ladies is gathered at the window, gazing out and conversing anxiously. The time
draws towards noon, when the clatter of a galloping horse's hoofs is heard echoing up the long
Potsdamer-Strasse, and presently turning into the Leipziger-Strasse reaches the open space commanded
by the ladies' outlook. It ceases before a Government building opposite them, and the rider disappears
into the courtyard.]

FIRST LADY
Yes: surely he is a courier from the field!

SECOND LADY
Shall we not hasten down, and take from him
The doom his tongue may deal us?

THIRD LADY
We shall catch
As soon by watching here as hastening hence
The tenour of his new. [They wait.] Ah, yes: see—see
The bulletin is straightway to be nailed!
He was, then, from the field....

[They wait on while the bulletin is affixed.]

SECOND LADY
I cannot scan the words the scroll proclaims;
Peer as I will, these too quick-thronging dreads
Bring water to the eyes. Grant us, good Heaven,
That victory be where she is needed most

To prove Thy goodness!... What do you make of it?

THIRD LADY [reading, through a glass]
"The battle strains us sorely; but resolve
May save us even now. Our last attack
Has failed, with fearful loss. Once more we strive."

[A long silence in the room. Another rider is heard approaching, above the murmur of the gathering citizens. The second lady looks out.]

SECOND LADY
A straggler merely he.... But they decide,
At last, to post his news, wild-winged or no.

THIRD LADY [reading again through her glass]
"The Duke of Brunswick, leading on a charge,
Has met his death-doom. Schmettau, too, is slain;
Prince William wounded. But we stand as yet,
Engaging with the last of our reserves."

[The agitation in the street communicates itself to the room. Some of the ladies weep silently as they wait, much longer this time. Another horseman is at length heard clattering into the Platz, and they lean out again with painful eagerness.]

SECOND LADY
An adjutant of Marshal Moellendorf's
If I define him rightly. Read—O read!—
Though reading draw them from their socket-holes
Use your eyes now!

THIRD LADY [glass up]
As soon as 'tis affixed....
Ah—this means much! The people's air and gait
Too well betray disaster. [Reading.] "Berliners,
The King has lost the battle! Bear it well.
The foremost duty of a citizen
Is to maintain a brave tranquillity.
This is what I, the Governor, demand
Of men and women now.... The King lives still."

[They turn from the window and sit in a silence broken only by monosyllabic words, hearing abstractedly the dismay without that has followed the previous excitement and hope.

The stagnation is ended by a cheering outside, of subdued emotional quality, mixed with sounds of grief. They again look forth. QUEEN LOUISA is leaving the city with a very small escort, and the populace seem overcome. They strain their eyes after her as she disappears. Enter fourth lady.]

FIRST LADY

How does she bear it? Whither does she go?

FOURTH LADY
She goes to join the King at Custrin, there
To abide events—as we. Her heroism
So schools her sense of her calamities
As out of grief to carve new queenliness,
And turn a mobile mien to statuesque,
Save for a sliding tear.

[The ladies leave the window severally.]

SPIRIT IRONIC
So the Will plays at flux and reflux still.
This monarchy, one-half whose pedestal
Is built of Polish bones, has bones home-made!
Let the fair woman bear it. Poland did.

SPIRIT OF THE YEARS
Meanwhile the mighty Emperor nears apace,
And soon will glitter at the city gates
With palpitating drums, and breathing brass,
And rampant joyful-jingling retinue.

[An evening mist cloaks the scene.]

SCENE VI

THE SAME

[It is a brilliant morning, with a fresh breeze, and not a cloud. The open Platz and the adjoining streets
are filled with dense crowds of citizens, in whose upturned faces curiosity has mastered consternation
and grief.

Martial music is heard, at first faint, then louder, followed by a trampling of innumerable horses and a
clanking of arms and accoutrements. Through a street on the right hand of the view from the windows
come troops of French dragoons heralding the arrival of BONAPARTE.

Re-enter the room hurriedly and cross to the windows several ladies as before, some in tears.]

FIRST LADY
The kingdom late of Prussia, can it be
That thus it disappears?—a patriot-cry,
A battle, bravery, ruin; and no more?

SECOND LADY

Thank God the Queen's gone!

THIRD LADY
To what sanctuary?
From earthquake shocks there is no sheltering cell!
—Is this what men call conquest? Must it close
As historied conquests do, or be annulled
By modern reason and the urbaner sense?—
Such issue none would venture to predict,
Yet folly 'twere to nourish foreshaped fears
And suffer in conjecture and in deed.—
If verily our country be dislimbed,
Then at the mercy of his domination
The face of earth will lie, and vassal kings
Stand waiting on himself the Overking,
Who ruling rules all; till desperateness
Sting and excite a bonded last resistance,
And work its own release.

SECOND LADY
He comes even now
From sacrilege. I learn that, since the fight,
In marching here by Potsdam yesterday,
Sans-Souci Palace drew his curious feet,
Where even great Frederick's tomb was bared to him.

FOURTH LADY
All objects on the Palace—cared for, kept
Even as they were when our arch-monarch died—
The books, the chair, the inkhorn, and the pen
He quizzed with flippant curiosity;
And entering where our hero's bones are urned
He seized the sword and standards treasured there,
And with a mixed effrontery and regard
Declared they should be all dispatched to Paris
As gifts to the Hotel des Invalides.

THIRD LADY
Such rodomontade is cheap: what matters it!

[A galaxy of marshals, forming Napoleon's staff, now enters the Platz immediately before the windows.
In the midst rides the EMPEROR himself. The ladies are silent. The procession passes along the front
until it reaches the entrance to the Royal Palace. At the door NAPOLEON descends from his horse and
goes into the building amid the resonant trumpetings of his soldiers and the silence of the crowd.]

SECOND LADY [impressed]
O why does such a man debase himself
By countenancing loud scurrility

Against a queen who cannot make reprise!
A power so ponderous needs no littleness—
The last resort of feeble desperates!

[Enter fifth lady.]

FIFTH LADY [breathlessly]
Humiliation grows acuter still.
He placards rhetoric to his soldiery
On their distress of us and our allies,
Declaring he'll not stack away his arms
Till he has choked the remaining foes of France
In their own gainful glut.—Whom means he, think you?

FIRST LADY
Us?

THIRD LADY
Russia? Austria?

FIFTH LADY
Neither: England.—Yea,
Her he still holds the master mischief-mind,
And marrer of the countries' quietude,
By exercising untold tyranny
Over all the ports and seas.

SECOND LADY
Then England's doomed!
When he has overturned the Russian rule,
England comes next for wrack. They say that know!...
Look—he has entered by the Royal doors
And makes the Palace his.—Now let us go!—
Our course, alas! is—whither?

[Exeunt ladies. The curtain drops temporarily.]

SEMICHORUS I OF IRONIC SPIRITS [aerial music]
Deeming himself omnipotent
With the Kings of the Christian continent,
To warden the waves was his further bent.

SEMICHORUS II
But the weaving Will from eternity,
[Hemming them in by a circling sea]
Evolved the fleet of the Englishry.

SEMICHORUS I

The wane of his armaments ill-advised,
At Trafalgar, to a force despised,
Was a wound which never has cicatrized.

SEMICHORUS II
This, O this is the cramp that grips!
And freezes the Emperor's finger-tips
From signing a peace with the Land of Ships.

CHORUS
The Universal-empire plot
Demands the rule of that wave-walled spot;
And peace with England cometh not!

THE SCENE REOPENS

[A lurid gloom now envelops the Platz and city; and Bonaparte is heard as from the Palace:

VOICE OF NAPOLEON
These monstrous violations being in train
Of law and national integrities
By English arrogance in things marine,
[Which dares to capture simple merchant-craft,
In honest quest of harmless merchandize,
For crime of kinship to a hostile power]
Our vast, effectual, and majestic strokes
In this unmatched campaign, enable me
To bar from commerce with the Continent
All keels of English frame. Hence I decree:—

SPIRIT OF RUMOUR
This outlines his renowned "Berlin Decree."
Maybe he meditates its scheme in sleep,
Or hints it to his suite, or syllables it
While shaping, to his scribes.

VOICE OF NAPOLEON
All England's ports to suffer strict blockade;
All traffic with that land to cease forthwith;
All natives of her isles, wherever met,
To be detained as windfalls of the war.
All chattels of her make, material, mould,
To be good prize wherever pounced upon:
And never a bottom hailing from her shores
But shall be barred from every haven here.
This for her monstrous harms to human rights,
And shameless sauciness to neighbour powers!

SPIRIT SINISTER
I spell herein that our excellently high-coloured drama is not played out yet!

SPIRIT OF THE YEARS
Nor will it be for many a month of moans,
And summer shocks, and winter-whitened bones.

[The night gets darker, and the Palace outlines are lost.]

SCENE VII

TILSIT AND THE RIVER NIEMEN

[The scene is viewed from the windows of BONAPARTE'S temporary quarters. Some sub-officers of his
suite are looking out upon it.

It is the day after midsummer, about one o'clock. A multitude of soldiery and spectators lines each bank
of the broad river which, stealing slowly north-west, bears almost exactly in its midst a moored raft of
bonded timber. On this as a floor stands a gorgeous pavilion of draped woodwork, having at each side,
facing the respective banks of the stream, a round-headed doorway richly festooned. The cumbersome
erection acquires from the current a rhythmical movement, as if it were breathing, and the breeze now
and then produces a shiver on the face of the stream.]

DUMB SHOW
On the south-west or Prussian side rides the EMPEROR NAPOLEON in uniform, attended by the GRAND
DUKE OF BERG, the PRINCE OF NEUFCHATEL, MARSHAL BESSIERES, DUROC Marshal of the Palace, and
CAULAINCOURT Master of the Horse. The EMPEROR looks well, but is growing fat. They embark on an
ornamental barge in front of them, which immediately puts off. It is now apparent to the watchers that
a precisely similar enactment has simultaneously taken place on the opposite or Russian bank, the chief
figure being the EMPEROR ALEXANDER—a graceful, flexible man of thirty, with a courteous manner and
good-natured face. He has come out from an inn on that side accompanied by the GRAND DUKE
CONSTANTINE, GENERAL BENNIGSEN, GENERAL OUWAROFF, PRINCE LABANOFF, and ADJUTANT-
GENERAL COUNT LIEVEN.

The two barges draw towards the raft, reaching the opposite sides of it about the same time, amidst
discharges of cannon. Each Emperor enters the door that faces him, and meeting in the centre of the
pavilion they formally embrace each other. They retire together to the screened interior, the suite of
each remaining in the outer half of the pavilion.

More than an hour passes while they are thus invisible. The French officers who have observed the
scene from the lodging of NAPOLEON walk about idly, and ever and anon go curiously to the windows,
again to watch the raft.

CHORUS OF THE YEARS [aerial music]
The prelude to this smooth scene—mark well!—were the shocks whereof the times gave token
Vaguely to us ere last year's snows shut over Lithuanian pine and pool,

Which we told at the fall of the faded leaf, when the pride of Prussia was bruised and broken,
And the Man of Adventure sat in the seat of the Man of Method and rigid Rule.

SEMICHORUS I OF THE PITIES
Snows incarnadined were thine, O Eylau, field of the wide white spaces,
And frozen lakes, and frozen limbs, and blood iced hard as it left the veins:
Steel-cased squadrons swathed in cloud-drift, plunging to doom through pathless places,
And forty thousand dead and near dead, strewing the early-lighted plains.
Friedland to these adds its tale of victims, its midnight marches and hot collisions,
Its plunge, at his word, on the enemy hooped by the bended river and famed Mill stream,
As he shatters the moves of the loose-knit nations to curb his exploitful soul's ambitions,
And their great Confederacy dissolves like the diorama of a dream.

DUMB SHOW [continues]
NAPOLEON and ALEXANDER emerge from their seclusion, and each is beheld talking to the suite of his
companion apparently in flattering compliment. An effusive parting, which signifies itself to be but
temporary, is followed by their return to the river shores amid the cheers of the spectators.

NAPOLEON and his marshals arrive at the door of his quarters and enter, and pass out of sight to other
rooms than that of the foreground in which the observers are loitering. Dumb show ends.

[A murmured conversation grows audible, carried on by two persons in the crowd beneath the open
windows. Their dress being the native one, and their tongue unfamiliar, they seem to the officers to be
merely inhabitants gossiping; and their voices continue unheeded.]

FIRST ENGLISH SPY (1) [below]
Did you get much for me to send on?

SECOND ENGLISH SPY
Much; and startling, too. "Why are we at war?" says Napoleon when they met.—"Ah—why!" said
t'other.—"Well," said Boney, "I am fighting you only as an ally of the English, and you are simply serving
them, and not yourself, in fighting me."—"In that case," says Alexander, "we shall soon be friends, for I
owe her as great a grudge as you."

FIRST SPY
Dammy, go that length, did they!

SECOND SPY
Then they plunged into the old story about English selfishness, and greed, and duplicity. But the climax
related to Spain, and it amounted to this: they agreed that the Bourbons of the Spanish throne should
be made to abdicate, and Bonaparte's relations set up as sovereigns instead of them.

FIRST SPY
Somebody must ride like hell to let our Cabinet know!

SECOND SPY

I have written it down in cipher, not to trust to memory, and to guard against accidents.—They also agree that France should have the Pope's dominions, Malta, and Egypt; that Napoleon's brother Joseph should have Sicily as well as Naples, and that they would partition the Ottoman Empire between them.

FIRST SPY
Cutting up Europe like a plum-pudding. Par nobile fratrum!

SECOND SPY
Then they worthy pair came to poor Prussia, whom Alexander, they say, was anxious about, as he is under engagements to her. It seems that Napoleon agrees to restore to the King as many of his states as will cover Alexander's promise, so that the Tsar may feel free to strike out in this new line with his new friend.

FIRST SPY
Surely this is but surmise?

SECOND SPY
Not at all. One of the suite overheard, and I got round him. There was much more, which I did not learn. But they are going to soothe and flatter the unfortunate King and Queen by asking them to a banquet here.

FIRST SPY
Such a spirited woman will never come!

SECOND SPY
We shall see. Whom necessity compels needs must: and she has gone through an Iliad of woes!

FIRST SPY
It is this Spanish business that will stagger England, by God! And now to let her know it,

FRENCH SUBALTERN [looking out above]
What are those townspeople talking about so earnestly, I wonder? The lingo of this place has an accent akin to English.

SECOND SUBALTERN
No doubt because the races are both Teutonic.

[The spies observe that they are noticed, and disappear in the crowd. The curtain drops.]

SCENE VIII

THE SAME

[The midsummer sun is low, and a long table in the aforeshown apartment is laid out for a dinner, among the decorations being bunches of the season's roses.

At the vacant end of the room [divided from the dining end by folding-doors, now open] there are discovered the EMPEROR NAPOLEON, the GRAND-DUKE CONSTANTINE, PRINCE HENRY OF PRUSSIA, the PRINCE ROYAL OF BAVARIA, the GRAND DUKE OF BERG, and attendant officers.

Enter the TSAR ALEXANDER. NAPOLEON welcomes him, and the twain move apart from the rest. BONAPARTE placing a chair for his visitor and flinging himself down on another.]

NAPOLEON
The comforts I can offer are not great,
Nor is the accommodation more than scant
That falls to me for hospitality;
But, as it is, accept.

ALEXANDER
It serves well.
And to unbrace the bandages of state
Is as clear air to incense-stifled souls.
What of the Queen?

NAPOLEON
She's coming with the King.
We have some quarter-hour to spare or more
Before their Majesties are timed for us.

ALEXANDER
Good. I would speak of them. That she should show here
After the late events, betokens much!
Abasement in so proud a woman's heart [His voice grows tremulous.]
Is not without a dash of painfulness.
And I beseech you, sire, that you hold out
Some soothing hope for her?

NAPOLEON
I have, already!—
Now, sire, to those affairs we entered on:
Strong friendship, grown secure, bids me repeat
That you have been much duped by your allies.

[ALEXANDER shows mortification.]

Prussia's a shuffler, England a self-seeker,
Nobility has shone in you alone.
Your error grew of over-generous dreams,
And misbeliefs by dullard ministers.
By treating personally we speed affairs
More in an hour than they in blundering months.
Between us two, henceforth, must stand no third.
There's peril in it, while England's mean ambition

Still works to get us skewered by the ears;
And in this view your chiefs-of-staff concur.

ALEXANDER
The judgment of my officers I share.

NAPOLEON
To recapitulate. Nothing can greaten you
Like this alliance. Providence has flung
My good friend Sultan Selim from his throne,
Leaving me free in dealings with the Porte;
And I discern the hour as one to end
A rule that Time no longer lets cohere.
If I abstain, its spoils will go to swell
The power of this same England, our annoy;
That country which enchains the trade of towns
With such bold reach as to monopolize,
Among the rest, the whole of Petersburg's—
Ay!—through her purse, friend, as the lender there!—
Shutting that purse, she may incite to—what?
Muscovy's fall, its ruler's murdering.
Her fleet at any minute can encoop
Yours in the Baltic; in the Black Sea, too;
And keep you snug as minnows in a glass!

Hence we, fast-fellowed by our mutual foes,
Seaward the British, Germany by land,
And having compassed, for our common good,
The Turkish Empire's due partitioning,
As comrades can conjunctly rule the world
To its own gain and our eternal fame!

ALEXANDER [stirred and flushed]

I see vast prospects opened!—yet, in truth,
Ere you, sire, broached these themes, their outlines loomed
Not seldom in my own imaginings;
But with less clear a vision than endows
So great a captain, statesman, philosoph,
As centre in yourself; whom had I known
Sooner by some few years, months, even weeks,
I had been spared full many a fault of rule.
—Now as to Austria. Should we call her in?

NAPOLEON
Two in a bed I have slept, but never three.

ALEXANDER

Ha-ha! Delightful. And, then nextly, Spain?

NAPOLEON
I lighted on some letters at Berlin,
Wherein King Carlos offered to attack me.
A Bourbon, minded thus, so near as Spain,
Is dangerous stuff. He must be seen to soon!...
A draft, then, of our treaty being penned,
We will peruse it later. If King George
Will not, upon the terms there offered him,
Conclude a ready peace, he can be forced.
Trumpet yourself as France's firm ally,
And Austria will fain to do the same:
England, left nude to such joint harassment,
Must shiver—fall.

ALEXANDER [with naive enthusiasm]
It is a great alliance!

NAPOLEON
Would it were one in blood as well as brain—
Of family hopes, and sweet domestic bliss!

ALEXANDER
Ah—is it to my sister you refer?

NAPOLEON
The launching of a lineal progeny
Has been much pressed upon me, much, of late,
For reasons which I will not dwell on now.
Staid counsellors, my brother Joseph, too,
Urge that I loose the Empress by divorce,
And re-wive promptly for the country's good.
Princesses even have been named for me!—
However this, to-day, is premature,
And 'twixt ourselves alone....

The Queen of Prussia must ere long be here:
Berthier escorts her. And the King, too, comes.
She's one whom you admire?

ALEXANDER [reddening ingenuously]
Yes.... Formerly
I had—did feel that some faint fascination
Vaguely adorned her form. And, to be plain,
Certain reports have been calumnious,
And wronged an honest woman.

NAPOLEON
As I knew!
But she is wearing thready: why, her years
Must be full one-and-thirty, if she's one.

ALEXANDER [quickly]
No, sire. She's twenty-nine. If traits teach more
It means that cruel memory gnaws at her
As fair inciter to that fatal war
Which broke her to the dust!... I do confess
[Since now we speak on't] that this sacrifice
Prussia is doomed to, still disquiets me.
Unhappy King! When I recall the oaths
Sworn him upon great Frederick's sepulchre,
And—and my promises to his sad Queen,
It pricks me that his realm and revenues
Should be stript down to the mere half they were!

NAPOLEON [cooly]
Believe me, 'tis but my regard for you
Which lets me leave him that! Far easier 'twere
To leave him none at all.

[He rises and goes to the window.]

But here they are.
No; it's the Queen alone, with Berthier
As I directed. Then the King will follow.

ALEXANDER
Let me, sire, urge your courtesy to bestow
Some gentle words on her?

NAPOLEON
Ay, ay; I will.

[Enter QUEEN LOUISA OF PRUSSIA on the arm of BERTHIER. She appears in majestic garments and with a smile on her lips, so that her still great beauty is impressive. But her eyes bear traces of tears. She accepts NAPOLEON'S attentions with the stormily sad air of a wounded beauty. Whilst she is being received the KING arrives. He is a plain, shy, honest-faced, awkward man, with a wrecked and solitary look. His manner to NAPOLEON is, nevertheless, dignified, and even stiff.

The company move into the inner half of the room, where the tables are, and the folding-doors being shut, they seat themselves at dinner, the QUEEN taking a place between NAPOLEON and ALEXANDER.]

NAPOLEON
Madame, I love magnificent attire;
But in the present instance can but note

That each bright knot and jewel less adorns
The brighter wearer than the wearer it!

QUEEN [with a sigh]
You praise one, sire, whom now the wanton world
Has learnt to cease from praising! But such words
From such a quarter are of worth no less.

NAPOLEON
Of worth as candour, madame; not as gauge.
Your reach in rarity outsoars my scope.
Yet, do you know, a troop of my hussars,
That last October day, nigh captured you?

QUEEN
Nay! Never a single Frenchman did I see.

NAPOLEON
Not less it was that you exposed yourself,
And should have been protected. But at Weimar,
Had you but sought me, 'twould have bettered you.

QUEEN
I had no zeal to meet you, sire, alas!

NAPOLEON [after a silence]
And how at Memel do you sport with time?

QUEEN
Sport? I!—I pore on musty chronicles,
And muse on usurpations long forgot,
And other historied dramas of high wrong!

NAPOLEON
Why con not annals of your own rich age?
They treasure acts well fit for pondering.

QUEEN
I am reminded too much of my age
By having had to live in it. May Heaven
Defend me now, and my wan ghost anon,
From conning it again!

NAPOLEON
Alas, alas!
Too grievous, this, for one who is yet a queen!

QUEEN

No; I have cause for vials more of grief.—
Prussia was blind in blazoning her power
Against the Mage of Earth!...
The embers of great Frederick's deeds inflamed her:
His glories swelled her to her ruining.
Too well has she been punished! [Emotion stops her.]

ALEXANDER [in a low voice, looking anxiously at her]
Say not so.
You speak as all were lost. Things are not thus!
Such desperation has unreason in it,
And bleeds the hearts that crave to comfort you.

NAPOLEON [to the King]
I trust the treaty, further pondered, sire,
Has consolations?

KING [curtly]
I am a luckless man;
And muster strength to bear my lucklessness
Without vain hope of consolations now.
One thing, at least, I trust I have shown you, sire
That I provoked not this calamity!
At Anspach first my feud with you began—
Anspach, my Eden, violated and shamed
By blushless tramplings of your legions there!

NAPOLEON
It's rather late, methinks, to talk thus now.

KING [with more choler]
Never too late for truth and plainspeaking!

NAPOLEON [blandly]
To your ally, the Tsar, I must refer you.
He was it, and not I, who tempted you
To push for war, when Eylau must have shown
Your every profit to have lain in peace.—
He can indemn; yes, much or small; and may.

KING [with a head-shake]
I would make up, would well make up, my mind
To half my kingdom's loss, could in such limb
But Magdeburg not lie. Dear Magdeburg,
Place of my heart-hold; THAT I would retain!

NAPOLEON
Our words take not such pattern as is wont

To grace occasions of festivity.

[He turns brusquely from the King. The banquet proceeds with a more general conversation. When finished a toast is proposed: "The Freedom of the Seas," and drunk with enthusiasm.]

SPIRIT SINISTER
Another hit at England and her tubs!
I hear harsh echoes from her chalky chines.

SPIRIT OF THE PITIES
O heed not England now! Still read the Queen.
One grieves to see her spend her pretty spells
Upon the man who has so injured her.

[They rise from table, and the folding-doors being opened they pass into the adjoining room.

Here are now assembled MURAT, TALLEYRAND, KOURAKIN, KALKREUTH, BERTHIER, BESSIERES, CAULAINCOURT, LABANOFF, BENNIGSEN, and others. NAPOLEON having spoken a few words here and there resumes his conversation with QUEEN LOUISA, and parenthetically offers snuff to the COUNTESS VOSS, her lady-in-waiting. TALLEYRAND, who has observed NAPOLEON'S growing interest in the QUEEN, contrives to get near him.]

TALLEYRAND [in a whisper]
Sire, is it possible that you can bend
To let one woman's fairness filch from you
All the resplendent fortune that attends
The grandest victory of your grand career?

[The QUEEN'S quick eye observes and flashes at the whisper, and she obtains a word with the minister.]

QUEEN [sarcastically]

I should infer, dear Monsieur Talleyrand,
Only two persons in the world regret
My having come to Tilsit.

TALLEYRAND
Madame, two?
Can any!—who may such sad rascals be?

QUEEN
You, and myself, Prince. [Gravely.] Yes! myself and you.

[TALLEYRAND'S face becomes impassive, and he does not reply. Soon the QUEEN prepares to leave, and NAPOLEON rejoins her.]

NAPOLEON [taking a rose from a vase]
Dear Queen, do pray accept this little token

As souvenir of me before you go?

[He offers her the rose, with his hand on his heart. She hesitates, but accepts it.]

QUEEN [impulsively, with waiting tears]
Let Magdeburg come with it, sire! O yes!

NAPOLEON [with sudden frigidity]
It is for you to take what I can give.
And I give this—no more. (2)

[She turns her head to hide her emotion, and withdraws. NAPOLEON steps up to her, and offers his arm. She takes it silently, and he perceives the tears on her cheeks. They cross towards the ante-room, away from the other guests.]

NAPOLEON [softly]
Still weeping, dearest lady! Why is this?

QUEEN [seizing his hand and pressing it]
Your speeches darn the tearings of your sword!—
Between us two, as man and woman now,
Is't even possible you question why!
O why did not the Greatest of the Age—
Of future ages—of the ages past,
This one time win a woman's worship—yea,
For all her little life!

NAPOLEON [gravely]
Know you, my Fair
That I—ay, I—in this deserve your pity.
Some force within me, baffling mine intent,
Harries me onward, whether I will or no.
My star, my star is what's to blame—not I.
It is unswervable!

QUEEN
Then now, alas!
My duty's done as mother, wife, and queen.—
I'll say no more—but that my heart is broken!

[Exeunt NAPOLEON, QUEEN, and LADY-IN-WAITING.]

SPIRIT OF THE YEARS
He spoke thus at the Bridge of Lodi. Strange,
He's of the few in Europe who discern
The working of the Will.

SPIRIT OF THE PITIES

If that be so,
Better for Europe lacked he such discerning!

[NAPOLEON returns to the room and joins TALLEYRAND.]

NAPOLEON [aside to his minister]
My God, it was touch-and-go that time, Talleyrand! She was within an ace of getting over me. As she stepped into the carriage she said in her pretty way, "O I have been cruelly deceived by you!" And when she sank down inside, not knowing I heard, she burst into sobs fit to move a statue. The Devil take me if I hadn't a good mind to stop the horses, jump in, give her a good kissing, and agree to all she wanted. Ha-ha, well; a miss is as good as a mile. Had she come sooner with those sweet, beseeching blue eyes of hers, who knows what might not have happened! But she didn't come sooner, and I have kept in my right mind.

[The RUSSIAN EMPEROR, the KING OF PRUSSIA, and other guests advance to bid adieu. They depart severally. When they are gone NAPOLEON turns to TALLEYRAND.]

Adhere, then, to the treaty as it stands:
Change not therein a single article,
But write it fair forthwith.

[Exeunt NAPOLEON, TALLEYRAND, and other ministers and officers in waiting.[

SHADE OF THE EARTH
Some surly voice afar I heard now
Of an enisled Britannic quality;
Wots any of the cause?

SPIRIT IRONIC
Perchance I do!
Britain is roused, in her slow, stolid style,
By Bonaparte's pronouncement at Berlin
Against her cargoes, commerce, life itself;
And now from out her water citadel
Blows counterblasting "Orders." Rumours tell.

RUMOUR I
"From havens of fierce France and her allies,
With poor or precious freight of merchandize
Whoso adventures, England pounds as prize!"

RUMOUR II
Thereat Napoleon names her, furiously,
Curst Oligarch, Arch-pirate of the sea,
Who shall lack room to live while liveth he!

CHORUS OF THE PITIES [aerial music]
And peoples are enmeshed in new calamity!

[Curtain of Evening Shades.]

[The view is from upper air, immediately over the region that lies between Bayonne on the north, Pampeluna on the south, and San Sebastian on the west, including a portion of the Cantabrian mountains. The month is February, and snow covers not only the peaks but the lower slopes. The roads over the passes are well beaten.]

DUMB SHOW
At various elevations multitudes of NAPOLEON'S soldiery, to the number of about thirty thousand, are discerned in a creeping progress across the frontier from the French to the Spanish side. The thin long columns serpentine along the roads, but are sometimes broken, while at others they disappear altogether behind vertical rocks and overhanging woods. The heavy guns and the whitey-brown tilts of the baggage-waggons seem the largest objects in the procession, which are dragged laboriously up the incline to the watershed, their lumbering being audible as high as the clouds.

Simultaneously the river Bidassoa, in a valley to the west, is being crossed by a train of artillery and another thirty thousand men, all forming part of the same systematic advance.

Along the great highway through Biscay the wondering native carters draw their sheep-skinned ox teams aside, to let the regiments pass, and stray groups of peaceable field-workers in Navarre look inquiringly at the marching and prancing progress.

Time passes, and the various northern strongholds are approached by these legions. Their governors emerge at a summons, and when seeming explanations have been given the unwelcome comers are doubtfully admitted.

The chief places to which entrance is thus obtained are Pampeluna and San Sebastian at the front of the scene, and far away towards the shining horizon of the Mediterranean, Figueras, and Barcelona.

Dumb Show concludes as the mountain mists close over.

[A private chamber is disclosed, richly furnished with paintings, vases, mirrors, silk hangings, gilded lounges, and several lutes of rare workmanship. The hour is midnight, the room being lit by screened candelabra. In the centre at the back of the scene is a large window heavily curtained.

GODOY and the QUEEN MARIA LUISA are dallying on a sofa. THE PRINCE OF PEACE is a fine handsome man in middle life, with curled hair and a mien of easy good-nature. The QUEEN is older, but looks younger in the dim light, from the lavish use of beautifying arts. She has pronounced features, dark eyes, low brows, black hair bound by a jewelled bandeau, and brought forward in curls over her forehead and temples, long heavy ear-rings, an open bodice, and sleeves puffed at the shoulders. A cloak and other mufflers lie on a chair beside her.]

GODOY
The life-guards still insist, Love, that the King
Shall not leave Aranjuez.

QUEEN
Let them insist.
Whether we stay, or whether we depart,
Napoleon soon draws hither with his host!

GODOY
He says he comes pacifically.... But no!

QUEEN
Dearest, we must away to Andalusia,
Thence to America when time shall serve.

GODOY
I hold seven thousand men to cover us,
And ships in Cadiz port. But then—the Prince
Flatly declines to go. He lauds the French
As true deliverers.

QUEEN
Go Fernando MUST!...
O my sweet friend, that we—our sole two selves—
Could but escape and leave the rest to fate,
And in a western bower dream out our days!—
For the King's glass can run but briefly now,
Shattered and shaken as his vigour is.—
But ah—your love burns not in singleness!
Why, dear, caress Josefa Tudo still?
She does not solve her soul in yours as I.
And why those others even more than her?...
How little own I in thee!

GODOY
Such must be.

I cannot quite forsake them. Don't forget
The same scope has been yours in former years.

QUEEN
Yes, Love; I know. I yield! You cannot leave them;
But if you ever would bethink yourself
How long I have been yours, how truly all
Those other pleasures were my desperate shifts
To soften sorrow at your absences,
You would be faithful to me!

GODOY
True, my dear.—
Yet I do passably keep troth with you,
And fond you with fair regularity;—
A week beside you, and a week away.
Such is not schemed without some risk and strain.—
And you agreed Josefa should be mine,
And, too, Thereza without jealousy!

[A noise is heard without.]

Ah, what means that?

[He jumps up from her side and crosses the room to a window, where he lifts the curtain cautiously.
The Queen follows him with a scared look.

QUEEN
A riot can it be?

GODOY
Let me put these out ere they notice them;
They think me at the Royal Palace yonder.

[He hastily extinguishes the candles except one taper, which he places in a recess, so that the room is in
shade. He then draws back the curtains, and she joins him at the window, where, enclosing her with his
arm, he and she look out together.

In front of the house a guard of hussars is stationed, beyond them spreading the Plaza or Square. On
the other side rises in the lamplight the white front of the Royal Palace. On the flank of the Palace is a
wall enclosing gardens, bowered alleys, and orange groves, and in the wall a small door.

A mixed multitude of soldiery and populace fills the space in front of the King's Palace, and they shout
and address each other vehemently. During a lull in their vociferations is heard the peaceful purl of the
Tagus over a cascade in the Palace grounds.]

QUEEN
Lingering, we've risked too long our chance of flight!

The Paris Terror will repeat it here.
Not for myself I fear. No, no; for thee! [She clings to him.]
If they should hurt you, it would murder me
By heart-bleedings and stabs intolerable!

GODOY [kissing her]
The first thought now is how to get you back
Within the Palace walls. Why would you risk
To come here on a night so critical?

QUEEN [passionately]
I could not help it—nay, I WOULD not help!
Rather than starve my soul I venture all.—
Our last love-night—last, maybe, of long years,
Why do you chide me now?

GODOY
Dear Queen, I do not:
I shape these sharp regrets but for your sake.
Hence you must go, somehow, and quickly too.
They think not yet of you in threatening thus,
But of me solely.... Where does your lady wait?

QUEEN
Below. One servant with her. They are true,
And can be let know all. But you—but you!

[Uproar continues.]

GODOY
I can escape. Now call them. All three cloak
And veil as when you came.

[They retreat into the room. QUEEN MARIA LUISA'S lady-in-waiting and servant are summoned. Enter both. All three then muffle themselves up, and GODOY prepares to conduct the QUEEN downstairs.]

QUEEN
Nay, now! I will not have it. We are safe;
Think of yourself. Can you get out behind?

GODOY
I judge so—when I have done what's needful here.—
The mob knows not the bye-door—slip across;
Thence around sideways.—All's clear there as yet.

[The QUEEN, her lady-in-waiting, and the servant go out hurriedly.]

GODOY looks again from the window. The mob is some way off, the immediate front being for the moment nearly free of loiterers; and the three muffled figures are visible, crossing without hindrance towards the door in the wall of the Palace Gardens. The instant they reach it a sentinel springs up, challenging them.]

GODOY
Ah—now they are doomed! My God, why did she come!

[A parley takes place. Something, apparently a bribe, is handed to the sentinel, and the three are allowed to slip in, the QUEEN having obviously been unrecognized. He breathes his relief.]

Now for the others. Then—ah, then Heaven knows!

[He sounds a bell and a servant enters.

Where is the Countess of Castillofiel?

SERVANT
She's looking for you, Prince.

GODOY
Find her at once.
Ah—here she is.—That's well.—Go watch the Plaza [to servant].

[GODOY'S mistress, the DONA JOSEFA TUDO, enters. She is a young and beautiful woman, the vivacity of whose large dark eyes is now clouded. She is wrapped up for flight. The servant goes out.]

JOSEFA [breathlessly]
I should have joined you sooner, but I knew
The Queen was fondling with you. She must needs
Come hampering you this night of all the rest,
As if not gorged with you at other times!

GODOY
Don't, pretty one! needless it is in you,
Being so well aware who holds my love.—
I could not check her coming, since she would.
You well know how the old thing is, and how
I am compelled to let her have her mind!

[He kisses her repeatedly.]

JOSEFA
But look, the mob is swelling! Pouring in
By thousands from Madrid—and all afoot.
Will they not come on hither from the King's?

GODOY

Not just yet, maybe. You should have sooner fled!
The coach is waiting and the baggage packed. [He again peers out.]
Yes, there the coach is; and the clamourers near,
Led by Montijo, if I see aright.
Yes, they cry "Uncle Peter!"—that means him.
There will be time yet. Now I'll take you down
So far as I may venture.

[They leave the room. In a few minutes GODOY, having taken her down, re-enters and again looks out. JOSEFA'S coach is moving off with a small escort of GODOY'S guards of honour. A sudden yelling begins, and the crowd rushes up and stops the vehicle. An altercation ensues.]

CROWD
Uncle Peter, it is the Favourite carrying off Prince Fernando.
Stop him!

JOSEFA [putting her head out of the coach]
Silence their uproar, please, Senor Count of Montijo! It is a lady only, the Countess of Castillofiel.

MONTIJO
Let her pass, let her pass, friends! It is only that pretty wench of his, Pepa Tudo, who calls herself a Countess. Our titles are put to comical uses these days. We shall catch the cock-bird presently!

[The DONA JOSEFA'S carriage is allowed to pass on, as a shout from some who have remained before the Royal Palace attracts the attention of the multitude, which surges back thither.]

CROWD [nearing the Palace]
Call out the King and the Prince. Long live the King! He shall not go. Hola! He is gone! Let us see him! He shall abandon Godoy!

[The clamour before the Royal Palace still increasing, a figure emerges upon a balcony, whom GODOY recognizes by the lamplight to be FERNANDO, Prince of Asturias. He can be seen waving his hand. The mob grows suddenly silent.]

FERNANDO [in a shaken voice]
Citizens! the King my father is in the palace with the Queen. He has been much tried to-day.

CROWD
Promise, Prince, that he shall not leave us. Promise!

FERNANDO
I do. I promise in his name. He has mistaken you, thinking you wanted his head. He knows better now.

CROWD
The villain Godoy misrepresented us to him! Throw out the Prince of Peace!

FERNANDO
He is not here, my friends.

CROWD
Then the King shall announce to us that he has dismissed him! Let us see him. The King; the King!

[FERNANDO goes in. KING CARLOS comes out reluctantly, and bows to their cheering. He produces a paper with a trembling hand.

KING [reading]
"As it is the wish of the people—"

CROWD
Speak up, your Majesty!

KING [more loudly]
"As it is the wish of the people, I release Don Manuel Godoy, Prince of Peace, from the posts of Generalissimo of the Army and Grand Admiral of the Fleet, and give him leave to withdraw whither he pleases."

CROWD
Huzza!

KING
Citizens, to-morrow the decree is to be posted in Madrid.

CROWD
Huzza! Long life to the King, and death to Godoy!

[KING CARLOS disappears from the balcony, and the populace, still increasing in numbers, look towards GODOY'S mansion, as if deliberating how to attack it. GODOY retreats from the window into the room, and gazing round him starts. A pale, worn, but placid lady, in a sombre though elegant robe, stands here in the gloom. She is THEREZA OF BOURBON, the Princess of Peace.]

PRINCESS
It is only your unhappy wife, Manuel. She will not hurt you!

GODOY [shrugging his shoulders]
Nor with THEY hurt YOU! Why did you not stay in the Royal Palace?
You would have been more comfortable there.

PRINCESS
I don't recognize why you should specially value my comfort. You have saved you real wives. How can it matter what happens to your titular one?

GODOY
Much, dear. I always play fair. But it being your blest privilege not to need my saving I was left free to practise it on those who did. [Mob heard approaching.] Would that I were in no more danger than you!

PRINCESS

Puf!

[He again peers out. His guard of hussars stands firmly in front of the mansion; but the life-guards from the adjoining barracks, who have joined the people, endeavour to break the hussars of GODOY. A shot is fired, GODOY'S guard yields, and the gate and door are battered in.

CROWD [without]
Murder him! murder him! Death to Manuel Godoy!

[They are heard rushing onto the court and house.]

PRINCESS
Go, I beseech you! You can do nothing for me, and I pray you to save yourself! The heap of mats in the lumber-room will hide you!

[GODOY hastes to a jib-door concealed by sham bookshelves, presses the spring of it, returns, kisses her, and then slips out.

His wife sits down with her back against the jib-door, and fans herself. She hears the crowd trampling up the stairs, but she does not move, and in a moment people burst in. The leaders are armed with stakes, daggers, and various improvised weapons, and some guards in undress appear with halberds.]

FIRST CITIZEN [peering into the dim light]
Where is he? Murder him! [Noticing the Princess.] Come, where is he?

PRINCESS
The Prince of Peace is gone. I know not wither.

SECOND CITIZEN
Who is this lady?

LIFE-GUARDSMAN
Manuel Godoy's Princess.

CITIZENS [uncovering]
Princess, a thousand pardons grant us!—you
An injured wife—an injured people we!
Common misfortune makes us more than kin.
No single hair of yours shall suffer harm.

[The PRINCESS bows.]

FIRST CITIZEN
But this, Senora, is no place for you,
For we mean mischief here! Yet first will grant
Safe conduct for you to the Palace gates,
Or elsewhere, as you wish

PRINCESS
My wish is nought.
Do what you will with me. But he's not here.

[Several of them form an escort, and accompany her from the room and out of the house. Those remaining, now a great throng, begin searching the room, and in bands invade other parts of the mansion.]

SOME CITIZENS [returning]
It is no use searching. She said he was not here, and she's a woman of honour.

FIRST CITIZEN [drily]
She's his wife.

[They begin knocking the furniture to pieces, tearing down the hangings, trampling on the musical instruments, and kicking holes through the paintings they have unhung from the walls. These, with clocks, vases, carvings, and other movables, they throw out of the window, till the chamber is a scene of utter wreck and desolation. In the rout a musical box is swept off a table, and starts playing a serenade as it falls on the floor. Enter the COUNT OF MONTIJO.]

MONTIJO
Stop, friends; stop this! There is no sense in it—
It shows but useless spite! I have much to say:
The French Ambassador, de Beauharnais,
Has come, and sought the King. And next Murat,
With thirty thousand men, half cavalry,
Is closing in upon our doomed Madrid!
I know not what he means, this Bonaparte;
He makes pretence to gain us Portugal,
But what want we with her? 'Tis like as not
His aim's to noose us vassals all to him!
The King will abdicate, and shortly too,
As those will live to see who live not long.—
We have saved our nation from the Favourite,
But who is going to save us from our Friend?

[The mob desists dubiously and goes out; the musical box upon the floor plays on, the taper burns to its socket, and the room becomes wrapt in the shades of night.]

SCENE III

LONDON: THE MARCHIONESS OF SALISBURY'S

[A large reception-room is disclosed, arranged for a conversazione. It is an evening in summer following, and at present the chamber is empty and in gloom. At one end is an elaborate device, representing

Britannia offering her assistance to Spain, and at the other a figure of Time crowning the Spanish Patriots' flag with laurel.]

SPIRIT OF THE YEARS
O clarionists of human welterings,
Relate how Europe's madding movement brings
This easeful haunt into the path of palpitating things!

RUMOURS [chanting]
The Spanish King has bowed unto the Fate
Which bade him abdicate:
The sensual Queen, whose passionate caprice
Has held her chambering with "the Prince of Peace,"
And wrought the Bourbon's fall,
Holds to her Love in all;
And Bonaparte has ruled that his and he
Henceforth displace the Bourbon dynasty.

II
The Spanish people, handled in such sort,
As chattels of a Court,
Dream dreams of England. Messengers are sent
In secret to the assembled Parliament,
In faith that England's hand
Will stouten them to stand,
And crown a cause which, hold they, bond and free
Must advocate enthusiastically.

SPIRIT OF THE YEARS
So the Will heaves through Space, and moulds the times,
With mortals for Its fingers! We shall see
Again men's passions, virtues, visions, crimes,
Obey resistlessly
The purposive, unmotived, dominant Thing
Which sways in brooding dark their wayfaring!

[The reception room is lighted up, and the hostess comes in. There arrive Ambassadors and their wives, the Dukes and Duchesses of RUTLAND and SOMERSET, the Marquis and Marchioness of STAFFORD, the Earls of STAIR, WESTMORELAND, GOWER, ESSEX, Viscounts and Viscountesses CRANLEY and MORPETH, Viscount MELBOURNE, Lord and Lady KINNAIRD, Baron de ROLLE, Lady CHARLES GRENVILLE, the Ladies CAVENDISH, Mr. and Mrs. THOMAS HOPE, MR. GUNNING, MRS. FITZHERBERT, and many other notable personages. Lastly, she goes to the door to welcome severally the PRINCE OF WALES, the PRINCES OF FRANCE, and the PRINCESS CASTELCICALA.]

LADY SALISBURY [to the Prince of Wales]
I am sorry to say, sir, that the Spanish Patriots are not yet arrived. I doubt not but that they have been delayed by their ignorance of the town, and will soon be here.

PRINCE OF WALES
No hurry whatever, my dear hostess. Gad, we've enough to talk about! I understand that the arrangement between our ministers and these noblemen will include the liberation of Spanish prisoners in this country, and the providing 'em with arms, to go back and fight for their independence.

LADY SALISBURY
It will be a blessed event if they do check the career of this infamous Corsican. I have just heard that that poor foreigner Guillet de la Gevrilliere, who proposed to Mr. Fox to assassinate him, died a miserable death a few days ago the Bicetre—probably by torture, though nobody knows. Really one almost wishes Mr. Fox had—. O here they are!

[Enter the Spanish Viscount de MATEROSA, and DON DIEGO de la VEGA. They are introduced by CAPTAIN HILL and MR. BAGOT, who escort them. LADY SALISBURY presents them to the PRINCE and others.]

PRINCE OF WALES
By gad, Viscount, we were just talking of 'ee. You had some adventures in getting to this country?

MATEROSA [assisted by Bagot as interpreter]
Sir, it has indeed been a trying experience for us. But here we are, impressed by a deep sense of gratitude for the signal marks of attachment your country has shown us.

PRINCE OF WALES
You represent, practically, the Spanish people?

MATEROSA
We are immediately deputed, sir,
By the Assembly of Asturias,
More sailing soon from other provinces.
We bring official writings, charging us
To clinch and solder Treaties with this realm
That may promote our cause against the foe.
Nextly a letter to your gracious King;
Also a Proclamation, soon to sound
And swell the pulse of the Peninsula,
Declaring that the act by which King Carlos
And his son Prince Fernando cede the throne
To whomsoever Napoleon may appoint,
Being an act of cheatery, not of choice,
Unfetters us from our allegiant oath.

MRS. FITZHERBERT
The usurpation began, I suppose, with the divisions in the Royal Family?

MATEROSA
Yes, madam, and the protection they foolishly requested from the Emperor; and their timid intent of flying secretly helped it on. It was an opportunity he had been awaiting for years.

MRS. FITZHERBERT
All brought about by this man Godoy, Prince of Peace!

PRINCE OF WALES
Dash my wig, mighty much you know about it, Maria! Why, sure, Boney thought to himself, "This Spain is a pretty place; 'twill just suit me as an extra acre or two; so here goes."

DON DIEGO [aside to Bagot]
This lady is the Princess of Wales?

BAGOT
Hsh! no, Senor. The Princess lives at large at Kensington and other places, and has parties of her own, and doesn't keep house with her husband. This lady is—well, really his wife, you know, in the opinion of many; but—

DON DIEGO
Ah! Ladies a little mixed, as they were at our Court! She's the Pepa Tudo to THIS Prince of Peace?

BAGOT
O no—not exactly that, Senor.

DON DIEGO
Ya, ya. Good. I'll be careful, my friend. You are not saints in England more than we are in Spain!

BAGOT
We are not. Only you sin with naked faces, and we with masks on.

DON DIEGO
Virtuous country!

DUCHESS OF RUTLAND
It was understood that Ferdinand, Prince of Asturias, was to marry a French princess, and so unite the countries peacefully?

MATEROSA
It was. And our credulous prince was tempted to meet Napoleon at Bayonne. Also the poor simple King, and the infatuated Queen, and Manuel Godoy.

DUCHESS OF RUTLAND
Then Godoy escaped from Aranjuez?

MATEROSA
Yes, by hiding in the garret. Then they all threw themselves upon Napoleon's protection. In his presence the Queen swore that the King was not Fernando's father! Altogether they form a queer little menagerie. What will happen to them nobody knows.

PRINCE OF WALES
And do you wish us to send an army at once?

MATEROSA
What we most want, sir, are arms and ammunition. But we leave the English Ministry to co-operate in its own wise way, anyhow, so as to sustain us in resenting these insults from the Tyrant of the Earth.

DUCHESS OF RUTLAND [to the Prince of Wales]
What sort of aid shall we send, sir?

PRINCE OF WALES
We are going to vote fifty millions, I hear. We'll whack him, and preserve your noble country for 'ee, Senor Viscount. The debate thereon is to come off to-morrow. It will be the finest thing the Commons have had since Pitt's time. Sheridan, who is open to it, says he and Canning are to be absolutely unanimous; and, by God, like the parties in his "Critic," when Government and Opposition do agree, their unanimity is wonderful! Viscount Materosa, you and your friends must be in the Gallery. O, dammy, you must!

MATEROSA
Sir, we are already pledged to be there.

PRINCE OF WALES
And hark ye, Senor Viscount. You will then learn what a mighty fine thing a debate in the English Parliament is! No Continental humbug there. Not but that the Court has a trouble to keep 'em in their places sometimes; and I would it had been one in the Lords instead. However, Sheridan says he has been learning his speech these two days, and has hunted his father's dictionary through for some stunning long words.—Now, Maria [to Mrs. Fitzherbert], I am going home.

LADY SALISBURY
At last, then, England will take her place in the forefront of this mortal struggle, and in pure disinterestedness fight with all her strength for the European deliverance God defend the right!

[The Prince of Wales leaves, and the other guests begin to depart.]

SEMICHORUS I OF THE YEARS [aerial music]
Leave this glib throng to its conjecturing,
And let four burdened weeks uncover what they bring!

SEMICHORUS II
The said Debate, to wit; its close in deed;
Till England stands enlisted for the Patriots' needs.

SEMICHORUS I
And transports in the docks gulp down their freight
Of buckled fighting-flesh, and gale-bound, watch and wait.

SEMICHORUS II
Till gracious zephyrs shoulder on their sails
To where the brine of Biscay moans its tragic tales.

CHORUS
Bear we, too, south, as we were swallow-vanned,
And mark the game now played there by the Master-hand!

[The reception-chamber is shut over by the night without, and the point of view rapidly recedes south, London and its streets and lights diminishing till they are lost in the distance, and its noises being succeeded by the babble of the Channel and Biscay waves.]

SCENE IV

MADRID AND ITS ENVIRONS

[The view is from the housetops of the city on a dusty evening in this July, following a day of suffocating heat. The sunburnt roofs, warm ochreous walls, and blue shadows of the capital, wear their usual aspect except for a few feeble attempts at decoration.]

DUMB SHOW
Gazers gather in the central streets, and particularly in the Puerta del Sol. They show curiosity, but no enthusiasm. Patrols of French soldiery move up and down in front of the people, and seem to awe them into quietude.

There is a discharge of artillery in the outskirts, and the church bells begin ringing; but the peals dwindle away to a melancholy jangle, and then to silence. Simultaneously, on the northern horizon of the arid, unenclosed, and treeless plain swept by the eye around the city, a cloud of dust arises, and a Royal procession is seen nearing. It means the new king, JOSEPH BONAPARTE.

He comes on, escorted by a clanking guard of four thousand Italian troops, and the brilliant royal carriage is followed by a hundred coaches bearing his suite. As the procession enters the city many houses reveal themselves to be closed, many citizens leave the route and walk elsewhere, while may of those who remain turn their backs upon the spectacle.

KING JOSEPH proceeds thus through the Plaza Oriente to the granite-walled Royal Palace, where he alights and is received by some of the nobility, the French generals who are in occupation there, and some clergy. Heralds emerge from the Palace, and hasten to divers points in the city, where trumpets are blown and the Proclamation of JOSEPH as KING OF SPAIN is read in a loud voice. It is received in silence.

The sunsets, and the curtain falls.

SCENE V

THE OPEN SEA BETWEEN THE ENGLISH COASTS AND THE SPANISH PENINSULA

[From high aloft, in the same July weather, and facing east, the vision swoops over the ocean and its coast-lines, from Cork Harbour on the extreme left, to Mondego Bay, Portugal, on the extreme right. Land's End and the Scilly Isles, Ushant and Cape Finisterre, are projecting features along the middle distance of the picture, and the English Channel recedes endwise as a tapering avenue near the centre.]

DUMB SHOW
Four groups of moth-like transport ships are discovered silently skimming this wide liquid plain. The first group, to the right, is just vanishing behind Cape Mondego to enter Mondego Bay; the second, in the midst, has come out from Plymouth Sound, and is preparing to stand down Channel; the third is clearing St. Helen's point for the same course; and the fourth, much further up Channel, is obviously to follow on considerably in the rear of the two preceding. A south-east wind is blowing strong, and, according to the part of their course reached, they either sail direct with the wind on their larboard quarter, or labour forward by tacking in zigzags.

SPIRIT OF THE PITIES
What are these fleets that cross the sea
From British ports and bays
To coasts that glister southwardly
Behind the dog-day haze?

RUMOURS [chanting]

SEMICHORUS I
They are the shipped battalions sent
To bar the bold Belligerent
Who stalks the Dancers' Land.
Within these hulls, like sheep a-pen,
Are packed in thousands fighting-men
And colonels in command.

SEMICHORUS II
The fleet that leans each aery fin
Far south, where Mondego mouths in,
Bears Wellesley and his aides therein,
And Hill, and Crauford too;
With Torrens, Ferguson, and Fane,
And majors, captains, clerks, in train,
And those grim needs that appertain—
The surgeons—not a few!
To them add twelve thousand souls
In linesmen that the list enrolls,
Borne onward by those sheeted poles
As war's red retinue!

SEMICHORUS I
The fleet that clears St. Helen's shore
Holds Burrard, Hope, ill-omened Moore,
Clinton and Paget; while

The transports that pertain to those
Count six-score sail, whose planks enclose
Ten thousand rank and file.

SEMICHORUS II
The third-sent ships, from Plymouth Sound,
With Acland, Anstruther, impound
Souls to six thousand strong.
While those, the fourth fleet, that we see
Far back, are lined with cavalry,
And guns of girth, wheeled heavily
To roll the routes along.

SPIRiT OF THE YEARS
Enough, and more, of inventories and names!
Many will fail; many earn doubtful fames.
Await the fruitage of their acts and aims.

DUMB SHOW [continuing]
In the spacious scene visible the far-separated groups of transports, convoyed by battleships, float on
before the wind almost imperceptibly, like preened duck-feathers across a pond. The southernmost
expedition, under SIR ARTHUR WELLESLEY, soon comes to anchor within the Bay of Mondego aforesaid,
and the soldiery are indefinitely discernible landing upon the beach from boats. Simultaneously the
division commanded by MOORE, as yet in the Chops of the channel, is seen to be beaten back by
contrary winds. It gallantly puts to sea again, and being joined by the division under ANSTRUTHER that
has set out from Plymouth, labours round Ushant, and stands to the south in the track of WELLESLEY.
The rearward transports do the same.

A moving stratum of summer cloud beneath the point of view covers up the spectacle like an awning.

SCENE VI

ST. CLOUD. THE BOUDOIR OF JOSEPHINE

[It is the dusk of evening in the latter summer of this year, and from the windows at the back of the
stage, which are still uncurtained, can be seen the EMPRESS with NAPOLEON and some ladies and
officers of the Court playing Catch-me-if-you-can by torchlight on the lawn. The moving torches throw
bizarre lights and shadows into the apartment, where only a remote candle or two are burning.

Enter JOSEPHINE and NAPOLEON together, somewhat out of breath. With careless suppleness she slides
down on a couch and fans herself. Now that the candle-rays reach her they show her mellow
complexion, her velvety eyes with long lashes, mouth with pointed corners and excessive mobility
beneath its duvet, and curls of dark hair pressed down upon the temples by a gold band.

The EMPEROR drops into a seat near her, and they remain in silence till he jumps up, knocks over some
nicknacks with his elbow, and begins walking about the boudoir.]

NAPOLEON [with sudden gloom]
These mindless games are very well, my friend;
But ours to-night marks, not improbably,
The last we play together.

JOSEPHINE [starting]
Can you say it!
Why raise that ghastly nightmare on me now,
When, for a moment, my poor brain had dreams
Denied it all the earlier anxious day?

NAPOLEON
Things that verge nigh, my simple Josephine,
Are not shoved off by wilful winking at.
Better quiz evils with too strained an eye
Than have them leap from disregarded lairs.

JOSEPHINE
Maybe 'tis true, and you shall have it so!—
Yet there's no joy save sorrow waived awhile.

NAPOLEON
Ha, ha! That's like you. Well, each day by day
I get sour news. Each hour since we returned
From this queer Spanish business at Bayonne,
I have had nothing else; and hence by brooding.

JOSEPHINE
But all went well throughout our touring-time?

NAPOLEON
Not so—behind the scenes. Our arms a Baylen
Have been smirched badly. Twenty thousand shamed
All through Dupont's ill-luck! The selfsame day
My brother Joseph's progress to Madrid
Was glorious as a sodden rocket's fizz!
Since when his letters creak with querulousness.
"Napoleon el chico" 'tis they call him—
"Napoleon the Little," so he says.
Then notice Austria. Much looks louring there,
And her sly new regard for England grows.
The English, next, have shipped an army down
To Mondego, under one Wellesley,
A man from India, and his march is south
To Lisbon, by Vimiero. On he'll go
And do the devil's mischief ere he is met
By unaware Junot, and chevyed back

To English fogs and fumes!

JOSEPHINE
My dearest one,
You have mused on worse reports with better grace
Full many and many a time. Ah—there is more!...
I know; I know!

NAPOLEON [kicking away a stool]
There is, of course; that worm
Time ever keeps in hand for gnawing me!—
The question of my dynasty—which bites
Closer and closer as the years wheel on.

JOSEPHINE
Of course it's that! For nothing else could hang
My lord on tenterhooks through nights and days;—
Or rather, not the question, but the tongues
That keep the question stirring. Nought recked you
Of throne-succession or dynastic lines
When gloriously engaged in Italy!
I was your fairy then: they labelled me
Your Lady of Victories; and much I joyed,
Till dangerous ones drew near and daily sowed
These choking tares within your fecund brain,—
Making me tremble if a panel crack,
Or mouse but cheep, or silent leaf sail down,
And murdering my melodious hours with dreads
That my late happiness, and my late hope,
Will oversoon be knelled!

NAPOLEON [genially nearing her]
But years have passed since first we talked of it,
And now, with loss of dear Hortense's son
Who won me as my own, it looms forth more.
And selfish 'tis in my good Josephine
To blind her vision to the weal of France,
And this great Empire's solidarity.
The grandeur of your sacrifice would gild
Your life's whole shape.

JOSEPHINE
Were I as coarse a wife
As I am limned in English caricature—
[Those cruel effigies they draw of me!]—
You could not speak more aridly.

NAPOLEON

Nay, nay!
You know, my comrade, how I love you still
Were there a long-notorious dislike
Betwixt us, reason might be in your dreads
But all earth knows our conjugality.
There's not a bourgeois couple in the land
Who, should dire duty rule their severance,
Could part with scanter scandal than could we.

JOSEPHINE [pouting]
Nevertheless there's one.

NAPOLEON
A scandal? What?

JOSEPHINE
Madame Walewska! How could you pretend
When, after Jena, I'd have come to you,
"The weather was so wild, the roads so rough,
That no one of my sex and delicate nerve
Could hope to face the dangers and fatigues."
Yes—so you wrote me, dear. They hurt not her!

NAPOLEON [blandly]
She was a week's adventure—not worth words!
I say 'tis France.—I have held out for years
Against the constant pressure brought on me
To null this sterile marriage.

JOSEPHINE [bursting into sobs]
Me you blame!
But how know you that you are not the culprit?

NAPOLEON
I have reason so to know—if I must say.
The Polish lady you have chosen to name
Has proved the fault not mine.

[JOSEPHINE sobs more violently.]

Don't cry, my cherished;
It is not really amiable of you,
Or prudent, my good little Josephine,
With so much in the balance.

JOSEPHINE
How—know you—
What may not happen! Wait a—little longer!

NAPOLEON [playfully pinching her arm]

O come, now, my adored! Haven't I already!
Nature's a dial whose shade no hand puts back,
Trick as we may! My friend, you are forty-three
This very year in the world—

[JOSEPHINE breaks out sobbing again.]

And in vain it is
To think of waiting longer; pitiful
To dream of coaxing shy fecundity
To an unlikely freak by physicking
With superstitious drugs and quackeries
That work you harm, not good. The fact being so,
I have looked it squarely down—against my heart!
Solicitations voiced repeatedly
At length have shown the soundness of their shape,
And left me no denial. You, at times,
My dear one, have been used to handle it.
My brother Joseph, years back, frankly gave
His honest view that something should be done;
And he, you well know, shows no ill tinct
In his regard of you.

JOSEPHINE
And what princess?

NAPOLEON
For wiving with? No thought was given to that,
She shapes as vaguely as the Veiled—

JOSEPHINE
No, no;
It's Alexander's sister, I'm full sure!—
But why this craze for home-made manikins
And lineage mere of flesh? You have said yourself
It mattered not. Great Caesar, you declared,
Sank sonless to his rest; was greater deemed
Even for the isolation. Frederick
Saw, too, no heir. It is the fate of such,
Often, to be denied the common hope
As fine for fulness in the rarer gifts
That Nature yields them. O my husband long,
Will you not purge your soul to value best
That high heredity from brain to brain
Which supersedes mere sequence of blood,
That often vary more from sire to son

Than between furthest strangers!...
Napoleon's offspring in his like must lie;
The second of his line be he who shows
Napoleon's soul in later bodiment,
The household father happening as he may!

NAPOLEON [smilingly wiping her eyes]
Little guessed I my dear would prove her rammed
With such a charge of apt philosophy
When tutoring me gay arts in earlier times!
She who at home coquetted through the years
In which I vainly penned her wishful words
To come and comfort me in Italy,
Might, faith, have urged it then effectually!
But never would you stir from Paris joys, [With some bitterness.]
And so, when arguments like this could move me,
I heard them not; and get them only now
When their weight dully falls. But I have said
'Tis not for me, but France—Good-bye an hour.

[Kissing her.]

I must dictate some letters. This new move
Of England on Madrid may mean some trouble.
Come, dwell not gloomily on this cold need
Of waiving private joy for policy.
We are but thistle-globes on Heaven's high gales,
And whither blown, or when, or how, or why,
Can choose us not at all!...
I'll come to you anon, dear: staunch Roustan
Will light me in.

[Exit NAPOLEON. The scene shuts in shadow.]

SCENE VII

VIMIERO

[A village among the hills of Portugal, about fifty miles north of Lisbon. Around it are disclosed, as ten on Sunday morning strikes, a blue army of fourteen thousand men in isolated columns, and red army of eighteen thousand in line formation, drawn up in order of battle. The blue army is a French one under JUNOT; the other an English one under SIR ARTHUR WELLESLEY—portion of that recently landed.

The August sun glares on the shaven faces, white gaiters, and white cross-belts of the English, who are to fight for their lives while sweating under a quarter-hundredweight in knapsack and pouches, and with firelocks heavy as putlogs. They occupy a group of heights, but their position is one of great danger, the land abruptly terminating two miles behind their backs in lofty cliffs overhanging the Atlantic. The French occupy the valleys in the English front, and this distinction between the two forces strikes the eye—the red army is accompanied by scarce any cavalry, while the blue is strong in that area.]

DUMB SHOW
The battle is begun with alternate moves that match each other like those of a chess opening. JUNOT makes an oblique attack by moving a division to his right; WELLESLEY moves several brigades to his left to balance it.

A column of six thousand French then climbs the hill against the English centre, and drives in those who are planted there. The English artillery checks its adversaries, and the infantry recover and charge the baffled French down the slopes. Meanwhile the latter's cavalry and artillery are attacking the village itself, and, rushing on a few squadrons of English dragoons stationed there, cut them to pieces. A dust is raised by this ado, and moans of men and shrieks of horses are heard. Close by the carnage the little Maceira stream continues to trickle unconcernedly to the sea.

On the English left five thousand French infantry, having ascended to the ridge and maintained a stinging musket-fire as sharply returned, are driven down by the bayonets of six English regiments. Thereafter a brigade of the French, the northernmost, finding that the others have pursued to the bottom and are resting after the effort, surprise them and bayonet them back to their original summit. The see-saw is continued by the recovery of the English, who again drive their assailants down.

The French army pauses stultified, till, the columns uniting, they fall back toward the opposite hills. The English, seeing that their chance has come, are about to pursue and settle the fortunes of the day. But a messenger dispatched from a distant group is marked riding up to the large-nosed man with a telescope and an Indian sword who, his staff around him, has been directing the English movements. He seems astonished at the message, appears to resent it, and pauses with a gloomy look. But he sends countermands to his generals, and the pursuit ends abortively.

The French retreat without further molestation by a circuitous march into the great road to Torres Vedras by which they came, leaving nearly two thousand dead and wounded on the slopes they have quitted.

Dumb Show ends and the curtain draws.

ACT THIRD

SCENE I

SPAIN. A ROAD NEAR ASTORGA

[The eye of the spectator rakes the road from the interior of a cellar which opens upon it, and forms the basement of a deserted house, the roof doors, and shutters of which have been pulled down and burnt for bivouac fires. The season is the beginning of January, and the country is covered with a sticky snow.

The road itself is intermittently encumbered with heavy traffic, the surface being churned to a yellow mud that lies half knee-deep, and at the numerous holes in the track forming still deeper quagmires.

In the gloom of the cellar are heaps of damp straw, in which ragged figures are lying half-buried, many of the men in the uniform of English regiments, and the women and children in clouts of all descriptions, some being nearly naked. At the back of the cellar is revealed, through a burst door, an inner vault, where are discernible some wooden-hooped wine-casks; in one sticks a gimlet, and the broaching-cork of another has been driven in. The wine runs into pitchers, washing-basins, shards, chamber-vessels, and other extemporized receptacles. Most of the inmates are drunk; some to insensibility.

So far as the characters are doing anything they are contemplating almost incessant traffic outside, passing in one direction. It includes a medley of stragglers from the Marquis of ROMANA'S Spanish forces and the retreating English army under SIR JOHN MOORE—to which the concealed deserters belong.]

FIRST DESERTER
Now he's one of the Eighty-first, and I'd gladly let that poor blade know that we've all that man can wish for here—good wine and buxom women. But if I do, we shan't have room for ourselves—hey?

[He signifies a man limping past with neither fire-lock nor knapsack. Where the discarded knapsack has rubbed for weeks against his shoulder-blades the jacket and shirt are fretted away, leaving his skin exposed.]

SECOND DESERTER
He may be the Eighty-firsht, or th' Eighty-second; but what I say is, without fear of contradiction, I wish to the Lord I was back in old Bristol again. I'd sooner have a nipperkin of our own real "Bristol milk" than a mash-tub full of this barbarian wine!

THIRD DESERTER
'Tis like thee to be ungrateful, after putting away such a skinful on't. I am as much Bristol as thee, but would as soon be here as there. There ain't near such willing women, that are strict respectable too, there as hereabout, and no open cellars.— As there's many a slip in this country I'll have the rest of my allowance now.

[He crawls on his elbows to one of the barrels, and turning on his back lets the wine run down his throat.]

FORTH DESERTER [to a fifth, who is snoring]
Don't treat us to such a snoaching there, mate. Here's some more coming, and they'll sight us if we don't mind!

[Enter without a straggling flock of military objects, some with fragments of shoes on, others bare-footed, many of the latter's feet bleeding. The arms and waists of some are clutched by women as tattered and bare-footed as themselves. They pass on.

The Retreat continues. More of ROMANA'S Spanish limp along in disorder; then enters a miscellaneous group of English cavalry soldiers, some on foot, some mounted, the rearmost of the latter bestriding a shoeless foundered creature whose neck is vertebrae and mane only. While passing it falls from exhaustion; the trooper extricates himself and pistols the animal through the head. He and the rest pass on.]

FIRST DESERTER [a new plashing of feet being heard]
Here's something more in order, or I am much mistaken. He cranes out.] Yes, a sergeant of the Forty-third, and what's left of their second battalion. And, by God, not far behind I see shining helmets. 'Tis a whole squadron of French dragoons!

[Enter the sergeant. He has a racking cough, but endeavours, by stiffening himself up, to hide how it is wasting away his life. He halts, and looks back, till the remains of the Forty-third are abreast, to the number of some three hundred, about half of whom are crippled invalids, the other half being presentable and armed soldiery.'

SERGEANT
Now show yer nerve, and be men. If you die to-day you won't have to die to-morrow. Fall in! [The miscellany falls in.] All invalids and men without arms march ahead as well as they can. Quick—maw-w-w-ch!

[Exeunt invalids, etc.]

Now! Tention! Shoulder-r-r—fawlocks!

[Order obeyed.]

[The sergeant hastily forms these into platoons, who prime and load, and seem preternaturally changed from what they were into alert soldiers.

Enter French dragoons at the left-back of the scene. The rear platoon of the Forty-third turns, fires, and proceeds. The next platoon covering them does the same. This is repeated several times, staggering the pursuers. Exeunt French dragoons, giving up the pursuit. The coughing sergeant and the remnant of the Forty-third march on.]

FOURTH DESERTER [to a woman lying beside him]
What d'ye think o' that, my honey? It fairly makes me a man again. Come, wake up! We must be getting along somehow. [He regards the woman more closely.] Why—my little chick? Look here, friends.

[They look, and the woman is found to be dead.]

If I didn't think that her poor knees felt cold!... And only an hour ago I swore to marry her!

[They remain silent. The Retreat continues in the snow without, now in the form of a file of ox-carts, followed by a mixed rabble of English and Spanish, and mules and muleteers hired by English officers to carry their baggage. The muleteers, looking about and seeing that the French dragoons gave been there, cut the bands which hold on the heavy packs, and scamper off with their mules.]

A VOICE [behind]

The Commander-in-Chief is determined to maintain discipline, and they must suffer. No more pillaging here. It is the worst case of brutality and plunder that we have had in this wretched time!

[Enter an English captain of hussars, a lieutenant, a guard of about a dozen, and three men as prisoner.]

CAPTAIN
If they choose to draw lots, only one need be made an example of.
But they must be quick about it. The advance-guard of the enemy is not far behind.

[The three prisoners appear to draw lots, and the one on whom the lot falls is blindfolded. Exeunt the hussars behind a wall, with carbines. A volley is heard and something falls. The wretched in the cellar shudder.]

FOURTH DESERTER
'Tis the same for us but for this heap of straw. Ah—my doxy is the only one of us who is safe and sound! [He kisses the dead woman.]

[Retreat continues. A train of six-horse baggage-waggons lumbers past, a mounted sergeant alongside. Among the baggage lie wounded soldiers and sick women.]

SERGEANT OF THE WAGGON-TRAIN
If so be they are dead, ye may as well drop 'em over the tail-board.
'Tis no use straining the horses unnecessary.

[Waggons halt. Two of the wounded who have just died are taken out, laid down by the roadside, and some muddy snow scraped over them. Exeunt waggons and sergeant.

An interval. More English troops pass on horses, mostly shoeless and foundered.

Enter SIR JOHN MOORE and officers. MOORE appears on the pale evening light as a handsome man, far on in the forties, the orbits of his dark eyes showing marks of deep anxiety. He is talking to some of his staff with vehement emphasis and gesture. They cross the scene and go on out of sight, and the squashing of their horses' hoofs in the snowy mud dies away.]

FIFTH DESERTER [incoherently in his sleep]
Poise fawlocks—open pans—right hands to pouch—handle ca'tridge—bring it—quick motion-bite top well off—prime—shut pans—cast about—load—

FIRST DESERTER [throwing a shoe at the sleeper]
Shut up that! D'ye think you are a 'cruity in the awkward squad still?

SECOND DESERTER
I don't know what he thinks, but I know what I feel! Would that I were at home in England again, where there's old-fashioned tipple, and a proper God A'mighty instead of this eternal 'Ooman and baby;—ay, at home a-leaning against old Bristol Bridge, and no questions asked, and the winter sun slanting friendly over Baldwin Street as 'a used to do! 'Tis my very belief, though I have lost all sure reckoning, that if I were there, and in good health, 'twould be New Year's day about now. What it is over here I don't know. Ay, to-night we should be a-setting in the tap of the "Adam and Eve"—lifting up the tune of

"The Light o' the Moon." 'Twer a romantical thing enough. 'A used to go som'at like this [he sings in a nasal tone]:—

"O I thought it had been day,
And I stole from here away;
But it proved to be the light o' the moon!"

[Retreat continues, with infantry in good order. Hearing the singing, one of the officers looks around, and detaching a patrol enters the ruined house with the file of men, the body of soldiers marching on. The inmates of the cellar bury themselves in the straw. The officer peers about, and seeing no one prods the straw with his sword.

VOICES [under the straw]

Oh! Hell! Stop it! We'll come out! Mercy! Quarter!

[The lurkers are uncovered.]

OFFICER
If you are well enough to sing bawdy songs, you are well enough to march. So out of it—or you'll be shot, here and now!

SEVERAL
You may shoot us, captain, or the French may shoot us, or the devil may take us; we don't care which! Only we can't stir. Pity the women, captain, but do what you will with us!

[The searchers pass over the wounded, and stir out those capable of marching, both men and women, so far as they discover them. They are pricked on by the patrol. Exeunt patrol and deserters in its charge.

Those who remain look stolidly at the highway. The English Rear-guard of cavalry crosses the scene and passes out. An interval. It grows dusk.]

SPIRIT IRONIC
Quaint poesy, and real romance of war!

SPIRIT OF THE PITIES
Mock on, Shade, if thou wilt! But others find
Poesy ever lurk where pit-pats poor mankind!

[The scene is cloaked in darkness.]

SCENE II

THE SAME

[It is nearly midnight. The fugitives who remain in the cellar having slept off the effects of the wine, are awakened by a new tramping of cavalry, which becomes more and more persistent. It is the French, who now fill the road. The advance-guard having passed by, DELABORDE'S division, LORGE'S division, MERLE'S division, and others, successively cross the gloom.

Presently come the outlines of the Imperial Guard, and then, with a start, those in hiding realize their situation, and are wide awake. NAPOLEON enters with his staff. He has just been overtaken by a courier, and orders those round him to halt.]

NAPOLEON
Let there a fire be lit: Ay, here and now.
The lines within these letters brook no pause
In mastering their purport.

[Some of the French approach the ruined house and, appropriating what wood is still left there, heap it by the roadside and set it alight. A mixed rain and snow falls, and the sputtering flames throw a glare all round.]

SECOND DESERTER [under his voice]
We be shot corpses! Ay, faith, we be! Why didn't I stick to England, and true doxology, and leave foreign doxies and their wine alone!... Mate, can ye squeeze another shardful from the cask there, for I feel my time is come!... O that I had but the barrel of that firelock I threw away, and that wasted powder to prime and load! This bullet I chaw to squench my hunger would do the rest!... Yes, I could pick him off now!

FIRST DESERTER
You lie low with your picking off, or he may pick off you! Thank God the babies are gone. Maybe we shan't be noticed, if we've but the courage to do nothing, and keep hid.

[NAPOLEON dismounts, approaches the fire, and looks around.]

NAPOLEON
Another of their dead horses here, I see.

OFFICER
Yes, sire. We have counted eighteen hundred odd
From Benavente hither, pistoled thus.
Some we'd to finish for them: headlong haste
Spared them no time for mercy to their brutes.
One-half their cavalry now tramps afoot.

NAPOLEON
And what's the tale of waggons we've picked up?

OFFICER
Spanish and all abandoned, some four hundred;
Of magazines and firelocks, full ten load;
And stragglers and their girls a numerous crew.

NAPOLEON
Ay, devil—plenty those! Licentious ones
These English, as all canting peoples are.—
And prisoners?

OFFICER
Seven hundred English, sire;
Spaniards five thousand more.

NAPOLEON
'Tis not amiss.
To keep the new year up they run away!
[He soliloquizes as he begins tearing open the dispatches.]
Nor Pitt nor Fox displayed such blundering
As glares in this campaign! It is, indeed,
Enlarging Folly to Foolhardiness
To combat France by land! But how expect
Aught that can claim the name of government
From Canning, Castlereagh, and Perceval,
Caballers all—poor sorry politicians—
To whom has fallen the luck of reaping in
The harvestings of Pitt's bold husbandry.

[He unfolds a dispatch, and looks for something to sit on. A cloak is thrown over a log, and he settles to reading by the firelight. The others stand round. The light, crossed by the snow-flakes, flickers on his unhealthy face and stoutening figure. He sinks into the rigidity of profound thought, till his features lour.]

So this is their reply! They have done with me!
Britain declines negotiating further—
Flouts France and Russia indiscriminately.
"Since one dethrones and keeps as prisoners
The most legitimate kings"—that means myself—
"The other suffers their unworthy treatment
For sordid interests"—that's for Alexander!...
And what is Georgy made to say besides?—
"Pacific overtures to us are wiles
Woven to unnerve the generous nations round
Lately escaped the galling yoke of France,
Or waiting so to do. Such, then, being seen,
These tentatives must be regarded now
As finally forgone; and crimson war
Be faced to its fell worst, unflinchingly."
—The devil take their lecture! What am I,
That England should return such insolence?

[He jumps up, furious, and walks to and fro beside the fire. By and by cooling he sits down again.]

Now as to hostile signs in Austria....
[He breaks another seal and reads.]
Ah,—swords to cross with her some day in spring!
Thinking me cornered over here in Spain
She speaks without disguise, the covert pact
'Twixt her and England owning now quite frankly,
Careless how works its knowledge upon me.
She, England, Germany: well—I can front them!
That there is no sufficient force of French
Between the Elbe and Rhine to prostrate her,
Let new and terrible experience
Soon disillude her of! Yea; she may arm:
The opportunity she late let slip
Will not subserve her now!

SPIRIT OF THE PITIES
Has he no heart-hints that this Austrian court,
Whereon his mood takes mould so masterful,
Is rearing naively in its nursery-room
A future wife for him?

SPIRIT OF THE YEARS
Thou dost but guess it,
And how should his heart know?

NAPOLEON [opening and reading another dispatch]
Now eastward. Ohe!—
The Orient likewise looms full somberly
The Turk declines pacifically to yield
What I have promised Alexander. Ah!...
As for Constantinople being his prize
I'll see him frozen first. His flight's too high!
And showing that I think so makes him cool. [Rises.]
Is Soult the Duke Dalmatia yet at hand?

OFFICER
He has arrived along the Leon road
Just now, your Majesty; and only waits
The close of your perusals.

[Enter SOULT, who is greeted by NAPOLEON.]

FIRST DESERTER
Good Lord deliver us from all great men, and take me back again to humble life! That's Marshal Soult the Duke of Dalmatia!

SECOND DESERTER

The Duke of Damnation for our poor rear, by the look on't!

FIRST DESERTER
Yes—he'll make 'em rub their poor rears before he has done with 'em! But we must overtake 'em to-morrow by a cross-cut, please God!

NAPOLEON [pointing to the dispatches]
Here's matter enough for me, Duke, and to spare.
The ominous contents are like the threats
The ancient prophets dealt rebellious Judah!
Austria we soon shall have upon our hands,
And England still is fierce for fighting on,—
Strange humour in a concord-loving land!
So now I must to Paris straight away—
At least, to Valladolid; so as to stand
More apt for couriers than I do out here
In this far western corner, and to mark
The veerings of these new developments,
And blow a counter-breeze....

Then, too, there's Lannes, still sweating at the siege
Of sullen Zaragoza as 'twere hell.
Him I must further counsel how to close
His twice too tedious battery.—You, then, Soult—
Ney is not yet, I gather, quite come up?

SOULT
He's near, sire, on the Benavente road;
But some hours to the rear I reckon, still.

NAPOLEON [pointing to the dispatches]
Him I'll direct to come to your support
In this pursuit and harassment of Moore
Wherein you take my place. You'll follow up
And chase the flying English to the sea.
Bear hard on them, the bayonet at their loins.
With Merle's and Mermet's corps just gone ahead,
And Delaborde's, and Heudelet's here at hand.
While Lorge's and Lahoussaye's picked dragoons
Will follow, and Franceschi's cavalry.
To Ney I am writing, in case of need,
He will support with Marchand and Mathieu.—
Your total thus of seventy thousand odd,
Ten thousand horse, and cannon to five score,
Should near annihilate this British force,
And carve a triumph large in history.
[He bends over the fire and makes some notes rapidly.]
I move into Astorga; then turn back,

[Though only in my person do I turn]
And leave to you the destinies of Spain.

SPIRIT OF THE YEARS
More turning may be here than he design.
In this small, sudden, swift turn backward, he
Suggests one turning from his apogee!

[The characters disperse, the fire sinks, and snowflakes and darkness blot out all.]

SCENE III

BEFORE CORUNA

[The town, harbour, and hills at the back are viewed from an aerial point to the north, over the lighthouse known as the Tower of Hercules, rising at the extremity of the tongue of land on which La Coruna stands, the open ocean being in the spectator's rear.

In the foreground the most prominent feature is the walled old town, with its white towers and houses, shaping itself aloft over the harbour. The new town, and its painted fronts, show bright below, even on this cloudy winter afternoon. Further off, behind the harbour—now crowded with British transports of all sizes—is a series of low broken hills, intersected by hedges and stone walls.

A mile behind these low inner hills is beheld a rocky chain of outer and loftier heights that completely command the former. Nothing behind them is seen but grey sky.

DUMB SHOW
On the inner hills aforesaid the little English army—a pathetic fourteen thousand of foot only—is just deploying into line: HOPE'S division is on the left, BAIRD'S to the right. PAGET with the reserve is in the hollow to the left behind them; and FRASER'S division still further back shapes out on a slight rise to the right.

This harassed force now appears as if composed of quite other than the men observed in the Retreat insubordinately straggling along like vagabonds. Yet they are the same men, suddenly stiffened and grown amenable to discipline by the satisfaction of standing to the enemy at last. They resemble a double palisade of red stakes, the only gaps being those that the melancholy necessity of scant numbers entails here and there.

Over the heads of these red men is beheld on the outer hills the twenty thousand French that have been pushed along the road at the heels of the English by SOULT. They have an ominous superiority, both in position and in their abundance of cavalry and artillery, over the slender lines of English foot. The left of this background, facing HOPE, is made up of DELABORDE'S and MERLE'S divisions, while in a deadly arc round BAIRD, from whom they are divided only by the village of Elvina, are placed MERMET'S division, LAHOUSSAYE'S and LORGE'S dragoons, FRANCESCHI'S cavalry, and, highest up of all, a formidable battery of eleven great guns that rake the whole British line.

It is now getting on for two o'clock, and a stir of activity has lately been noticed along the French front. Three columns are discerned descending from their position, the first towards the division of SIR DAVID BAIRD, the weakest point in the English line, the next towards the centre, the third towards the left. A heavy cannonade from the battery supports this advance.

The clash ensues, the English being swept down in swathes by the enemy's artillery. The opponents meet face to face at the village in the valley between them, and the fight there grows furious.

SIR JOHN MOORE is seen galloping to the front under the gloomy sky.

SPIRIT OF THE PITIES
I seem to vision in San Carlos' garden,
That rises salient in the upper town,
His name, and date, and doing, set within
A filmy outline like a monument,
Which yet is but the insubstantial air.

SPIRIT OF THE YEARS
Read visions as conjectures; not as more.

When MOORE arrives at the front, FRASER and PAGET move to the right, where the English are most sorely pressed. A grape-shot strikes off BAIRD'S arm. There is a little confusion, and he is borne to the rear; while MAJOR NAPIER disappears, a prisoner.

Intelligence of these misfortunes is brought to SIR JOHN MOORE. He goes further forward, and precedes in person the Forty-second regiment and a battalion of the Guards who, with fixed bayonets, bear the enemy back, MOORE'S gestures in cheering them being notably energetic. Pursuers, pursued, and SIR JOHN himself pass out of sight behind the hill. Dumb Show ends.

[The point of vision descends to the immediate rear of the English position. The early January evening has begun to spread its shades, and shouts of dismay are heard from behind the hill over which MOORE and the advancing lines have vanished.

Straggling soldiers cross in the gloom.]

FIRST STRAGGLER
He's struck by a cannon-ball, that I know; but he's not killed, that I pray God A'mighty.

SECOND STRAGGLER
Better he were. His shoulder is knocked to a bag of splinters. As Sir David was wounded, Sir John was anxious that the right should not give way, and went forward to keep it firm.

FIRST STRAGGLER
He didn't keep YOU firm, howsomever.

SECOND STRAGGLER
Nor you, for that matter.

FIRST STRAGGLER
Well, 'twas a serious place for a man with no priming-horn, and a character to lose, so I judged it best to fall to the rear by lying down. A man can't fight by the regulations without his priming-horn, and I am none of your slovenly anyhow fighters.

SECOND STRAGGLER
'Nation, having dropped my flit-pouch, I was the same. If you'd had your priming-horn, and I my flints, mind ye, we should have been there now? Then, forty-whory, that we are not is the fault o' Government for not supplying new ones from the reserve!

FIRST STRAGGLER
What did he say as he led us on?

SECOND STRAGGLER
"Forty-second, remember Egypt!" I heard it with my own ears. Yes, that was his strict testament.

FIRST STRAGGLER
"Remember Egypt." Ay, and I do, for I was there!... Upon my salvation, here's for back again, whether or no!

SECOND STRAGGLER
But here. "Forty-second, remember Egypt," he said in the very eye of that French battery playing through us. And the next omen was that he was struck off his horse, and fell on his back to the ground. I remembered Egypt, and what had just happened too, so thorough well that I remembered the way over this wall!—Captain Hardinge, who was close to him, jumped off his horse, and he and one in the ranks lifted him, and are now bringing him along.

FIRST STRAGGLER
Nevertheless, here's for back again, come what will. Remember Egypt! Hurrah!

[Exit First straggler. Second straggler ponders, then suddenly follows First. Enter COLONEL ANDERSON and others hastily.]

AN OFFICER
Now fetch a blanker. He must be carried in.

[Shouts heard.]

COLONEL ANDERSON
That means we are gaining ground! Had fate but left
This last blow undecreed, the hour had shone
A star amid these girdling days of gloom!

[Exit. Enter in the obscurity six soldiers of the Forty-second bearing MOORE on their joined hands. CAPTAIN HARDINGE walks beside and steadies him. He is temporarily laid down in the shelter of a wall, his left shoulder being pounded away, the arm dangling by a shred of flesh.

Enter COLONEL GRAHAM and CAPTAIN WOODFORD.]

GRAHAM
The wound is more than serious, Woodford, far.
Ride for a surgeon—one of those, perhaps,
Who tend Sir David Baird? [Exit Captain Woodford.]
His blood throbs forth so fast, that I have dark fears
He'll drain to death ere anything can be done!

HARDINGE
I'll try to staunch it—since no skill's in call.

[He takes off his sash and endeavours to bind the wound with it. MOORE smiles and shakes his head.]

There's not much checking it! Then rent's too gross.
A dozen lives could pass that thoroughfare!

[Enter a soldier with a blanket. They lift MOORE into it. During the operation the pommel of his sword, which he still wears, is accidentally thrust into the wound.]

I'll loose the sword—it bruises you, Sir John.

[He begins to unbuckle it.]

MOORE
No. Let it be! One hurt more matters not.
I wish it to go off the field with me.

HARDINGE
I like the sound of that. It augurs well
For your much-hoped recovery.

MOORE [looking sadly at his wound]
Hardinge, no:
Nature is nonplussed there! My shoulder's gone,
And this left side laid open to my lungs.
There's but a brief breath now for me, at most....
Could you—move me along—that I may glimpse
Still how the battle's going?

HARDINGE
Ay, Sir John—
A few yard higher up, where we can see.

[He is borne in the blanket a little way onward, and lifted so
that he can view the valley and the action.]

MOORE [brightly]

They seem to be advancing. Yes, it is so!

[Enter SIR JOHN HOPE.]

Ah, Hope!—I am doing badly here enough;
But they are doing rarely well out there. [Presses HOPE'S hand.]
Don't leave! my speech may flag with this fierce pain,
But you can talk to me.—Are the French checked?

HOPE
My dear friend, they are borne back steadily.

MOORE [his voice weakening]
I hope England—will be satisfied—
I hope my native land—will do me justice!...
I shall be blamed for sending Craufurd off
Along the Orense road. But had I not,
Bonaparte would have headed us that way....

HOPE
O would that Soult had but accepted battle
By Lugo town! We should have crushed him there.

MOORE
Yes... yes.—But it has never been my lot
To owe much to good luck; nor was it then.
Good fortune has been mine, but [bitterly] mostly so
By the exhaustion of all shapes of bad!...
Well, this does not become a dying man;
And others have been chastened more than I
By Him who holds us in His hollowed hand!...

I grieve for Zaragoza, if, as said,
The siege goes sorely with her, which it must.
I heard when at Dahagun that late day
That she was holding out heroically.
But I must leave such now.—You'll see my friends
As early as you can? Tell them the whole;
Say to my mother.... [His voice fails.]
Hope, Hope, I have so much to charge you with,
But weakness clams my tongue!... If I must die
Without a word with Stanhope, ask him, Hope,
To—name me to his sister. You may know
Of what there was between us?...
Is Colonel Graham well, and all my aides?
My will I have made—it is in Colborne's charge
With other papers.

HOPE
He's now coming up.

[Enter MAJOR COLBORNE, principal aide-de-camp.]

MOORE
Are the French beaten, Colborne, or repulsed?
Alas! you see what they have done too me!

COLBORNE
I do, Sir John: I am more than sad thereat!
In brief time now the surgeon will be here.
The French retreat—pushed from Elvina far.

MOORE
That's good! Is Paget anywhere about?

COLBORNE
He's at the front, Sir John.

MOORE
Remembrance to him!

[Enter two surgeons.]

Ah, doctors,—you can scarcely mend up me.—
And yet I feel so tough—I have feverish fears
My dying will waste a long and tedious while;
But not too long, I hope!

SURGEONS [after a hasty examination]
You must be borne
In to your lodgings instantly, Sir John.
Please strive to stand the motion—if you can;
They will keep step, and bear you steadily.

MOORE
Anything.... Surely fainter ebbs that fire?

COLBORNE
Yes: we must be advancing everywhere:
Colbert their General, too, they have lost, I learn.

[They lift him by stretching their sashes under the blanket, and begin moving off. A light waggon enters.]

MOORE
Who's in that waggon?

HARDINGE
Colonel Wynch, Sir John.
He's wounded, but he urges you to take it.

MOORE
No. I will not. This suits.... Don't come with me;
There's more for you to do out here as yet. [Cheerful shouts.]
A-ha! 'Tis THIS way I have wished to die!

[Exeunt slowly in the twilight MOORE, bearers, surgeons, etc., towards Coruna. The scene darkens.]

SCENE IV

CORUNA. NEAR THE RAMPARTS

[It is just before dawn on the following morning, objects being still indistinct. The features of the elevated enclosure of San Carlos can be recognized in dim outline, and also those of the Old Town of Coruna around, though scarcely a lamp is shining. The numerous transports in the harbour beneath have still their riding-lights burning.

In a nook of the town walls a lantern glimmers. Some English soldiers of the Ninth regiment are hastily digging a grave there with extemporized tools.]

A VOICE [from the gloom some distance off]
"I am the resurrection and the life, saith the Lord: he that
believeth in me, though he were dead, yet shall he live."

[The soldiers look up, and see entering at the further end of the patch of ground a slow procession. It advances by the light of lanterns in the hands of some members of it. At moments the fitful rays fall upon bearers carrying a coffinless body rolled in a blanket, with a military cloak roughly thrown over by way of pall. It is brought towards the incomplete grave, and followed by HOPE, GRAHAM, ANDERSON, COLBORNE, HARDINGE, and several aides-de-camp, a chaplain preceding.]

FIRST SOLDIER
They are here, almost as quickly as ourselves.
There is no time to dig much deeper now:
Level a bottom just as far's we've got.
He'll couch as calmly in this scrabbled hole
As in a royal vault!

SECOND SOLDIER
Would it had been a foot deeper, here among foreigners, with strange manures manufactured out of no one knows what! Surely we can give him another six inches?

FIRST SOLDIER

There is no time. Just make the bottom true.

[The meagre procession approaches the spot, and waits while the half-dug grave is roughly finished by the men of the Ninth. They step out of it, and another of them holds a lantern to the chaplain's book. The winter day slowly dawns.]

CHAPLAIN
"Man that is born of a woman hath but a short time to live, and is full of misery. He cometh up, and is cut down, like a flower; he fleeth as it were a shadow, and never continueth in one stay."

[A gun is fired from the French battery not far off; then another. The ships in the harbour take in their riding lights.]

COLBORNE [in a low voice]
I knew that dawn would see them open fire.

HOPE
We must perforce make swift use of out time.
Would we had closed our too sad office sooner!

[As the body is lowered another discharge echoes. They glance gloomily at the heights where the French are ranged, and then into the grave.]

CHAPLAIN
"We therefore commit his body to the ground. Earth to earth, ashes to ashes, dust to dust."

[Another gun.]

[A spent ball falls not far off. They put out their lanterns. Continued firing, some shot splashing into the harbour below them.]

HOPE
In mercy to the living, who are thrust
Upon our care for their deliverance,
And run much hazard till they are embarked,
We must abridge these duties to the dead,
Who will not mind be they abridged or no.

HARDINGE
And could he mind, would be the man to bid it....

HOPE
We shall do well, then, curtly to conclude
These mutilated prayers—our hurried best!—
And what's left unsaid, feel.

CHAPLAIN [his words broken by the cannonade]

".... We give Thee hearty thanks for that it hath pleased Thee to deliver this our brother out of the miseries of this sinful world.... Who also hath taught us not to be sorry, as men without hope, for them that sleep in Him.... Grant this, through Jesus Christ our Mediator and Redeemer."

OFFICERS AND SOLDIERS
Amen!

[The diggers of the Ninth hastily fill in the grave, and the scene shuts as the mournful figures retire.]

SCENE V

VIENNA. A CAFE IN THE STEPHANS-PLATZ

[An evening between light and dark is disclosed, some lamps being lit. The huge body and tower of St. Stephen's rise into the sky some way off, the western gleam still touching the upper stonework. Groups of people are seated at the tables, drinking and reading the newspapers. One very animated group, which includes an Englishman, is talking loudly. A citizen near looks up from his newspaper.]

CITIZEN [to the Englishman]
I read, sir, here, the troubles you discuss
Of your so gallant army under Moore.
His was a spirit baffled but not quelled,
And in his death there shone a stoicism
That lent retreat the rays of victory.

ENGLISHMAN
It was so. While men chide they will admire him,
And frowning, praise. I could nigh prophesy
That the unwonted crosses he has borne
In his career of sharp vicissitude
Will tinct his story with a tender charm,
And grant the memory of his strenuous feats
As long a lease within the minds of men
As conquerors hold there.—Does the sheet give news
Of how the troops reached home?

CITIZEN [looking up again at the paper]
Yes; from your press
It quotes that they arrived at Plymouth Sound
Mid dreadful weather and much suffering.
It states they looked the very ghosts of men,
So heavily had hunger told on them,
And the fatigues and toils of the retreat.
Several were landed dead, and many died
As they were borne along. At Portsmouth, too,
Sir David Baird, still helpless from his wound,

Was carried in a cot, sheet-pale and thin,
And Sir John Hope, lank as a skeleton.—
Thereto is added, with authority,
That a new expedition soon will fit,
And start again for Spain.

ENGLISHMAN
I have heard as much.

CITIZEN
You'll do it next time, sir. And so shall we!

SECOND CITIZEN [regarding the church tower opposite]
You witnessed the High Service over there
They held this morning? [To the Englishman.]

ENGLISHMAN
Ay; I did get in;
Though not without hard striving, such the throng;
But travellers roam to waste who shyly roam
And I pushed like the rest.

SECOND CITIZEN
Our young Archduchess
Maria Louisa was, they tell me, present?

ENGLISHMAN
O yes: the whole Imperial family,
And when the Bishop called all blessings down
Upon the Landwehr colours there displayed,
Enthusiasm touched the sky—she sharing it.

SECOND CITIZEN
Commendable in her, and spirited,
After the graceless insults to the Court
The Paris journals flaunt—not voluntarily,
But by his ordering. Magician-like
He holds them in his fist, and at his squeeze
They bubble what he wills!... Yes, she's a girl
Of patriotic build, and hates the French.
Quite lately she was overheard to say
She had met with most convincing auguries
That this year Bonaparte was starred to die.

ENGLISHMAN
Your arms must render its fulfilment sure.

SECOND CITIZEN

Right! And we have the opportunity,
By upping to the war in suddenness,
And catching him unaware. The pink and flower
Of all his veteran troops are now in Spain
Fully engaged with yours; while those he holds
In Germany are scattered far and wide.

FIRST CITIZEN [looking up again from his newspaper]
I see here that he vows and guarantees
Inviolate bounds to all our territories
If we but pledge to carry out forthwith
A prompt disarmament. Since that's his price
Hell burn his guarantees! Too long he has fooled us.
[To the Englishman] I drink, sir, to your land's consistency.
While we and all the kindred Europe States
Alternately have wooed and warred him,
You have not bent to blowing hot and cold,
But held you sturdily inimical!

ENGLISHMAN [laughing]
Less Christian-like forgiveness mellows us
Than Continental souls! [They drink.]

[A band is heard in a distant street, with shouting. Enter third and fourth citizens, followed by others.]

FIRST CITIZEN
More news afloat?

THIRD AND FOURTH CITIZENS
Yea; an announcement that the Archduke Charles
Is given the chief command.

FIRST, SECOND, ETC., CITIZENS
Huzza! Right so!

[A clinking of glasses, rising from seats, and general enthusiasm.]

SECOND CITIZEN
If war had not so patly been declared,
Our howitzers and firelocks of themselves
Would have gone off to shame us! This forenoon
Some of the Landwehr met me; they are hot
For setting out, though but few months enrolled.

ENGLISHMAN
That moves reflection somewhat. They are young
For measuring with the veteran file of France!

FIRST CITIZEN
Napoleon's army swarms with tender youth,
His last conscription besomed into it
Thousands of merest boys. But he contrives
To mix them in the field with seasoned frames.

SECOND CITIZEN
The sadly-seen mistake this country made
Was that of grounding hostile arms at all.
We should have fought irreconcilably—
Have been consistent as the English are.
The French are our hereditary foes,
And this adventurer of the saucy sword,
This sacrilegious slighter of our shrines,
Stands author of all our ills...
Our harvest fields and fruits he trample on,
Accumulating ruin in our land.
Think of what mournings in the last sad war
'Twas his to instigate and answer for!
Time never can efface the glint of tears
In palaces, in shops, in fields, in cots,
From women widowed, sonless, fatherless,
That then oppressed our eyes. There is no salve
For such deep harrowings but to fight again;
The enfranchisement of Europe hangs thereon,
And long she has lingered for the sign to crush him:
That signal we have given; the time is come!

[Thumping on the table.]

FIFTH CITIZEN [at another table, looking up from his paper and speaking across]
I see that Russia has declined to aid us,
And says she knows that Prussia likewise must;
So that the mission of Prince Schwarzenberg
To Alexander's Court has closed in failure.

THIRD CITIZEN
Ay—through his being honest—fatal sin!—
Probing too plainly for the Emperor's ears
His ominous friendship with Napoleon.

ENGLISHMAN
Some say he was more than honest with the Tsar;
Hinting that his becoming an ally
Makes him accomplice of the Corsican
In the unprincipled dark overthrow
Of his poor trusting childish Spanish friends—
Which gave the Tsar offence.

THIRD CITIZEN
And our best bid—
The last, most delicate dish—a tastelessness.

FIRST CITIZEN
What was Prince Schwarzenberg's best bid, I pray?

THIRD CITIZEN
The offer of the heir of Austria's hand
For Alexander's sister the Grand-Duchess.

ENGLISHMAN
He could not have accepted, if or no:
She is inscribed as wife for Bonaparte.

FIRST CITIZEN
I doubt that text!

ENGLISHMAN
Time's context soon will show.

SECOND CITIZEN
The Russian Cabinet can not for long
Resist the ardour of the Russian ranks
To march with us the moment we achieve
Our first loud victory!

[A band is heard playing afar, and shouting People are seen hurrying past in the direction of the sounds. Enter sixth citizen.]

SIXTH CITIZEN
The Archduke Charles
Is passing the Ringstrasse just by now,
His regiment at his heels!

[The younger sitters jump up with animation, and go out, the elder mostly remaining.]

SECOND CITIZEN
Realm never faced
The grin of a more fierce necessity
For horrid war, than ours at this tense time!

[The sounds of band-playing and huzzaing wane away. Citizens return.]

FIRST CITIZEN
More news, my friends, of swiftly swelling zeal?

RE-ENTERED CITIZENS
Ere passing down the Ring, the Archduke paused
And gave the soldiers speech, enkindling them
As sunrise a confronting throng of panes
That glaze a many-windowed east facade:
Hot volunteers vamp in from vill and plain—
More than we need in the furthest sacrifice!

FIRST, SECOND, ETC., CITIZENS
Huzza! Right so! Good! Forwards! God be praised!

[They stand up, and a clinking of glasses follows, till they subside to quietude and a reperusal of newspapers. Nightfall succeeds. Dancing-rooms are lit up in an opposite street, and dancing begins. The figures are seen gracefully moving round to the throbbing strains of a string-band, which plays a new waltzing movement with a warlike name, soon to spread over Europe. The dancers sing patriotic words as they whirl. The night closes over.]

ACT FOURTH

SCENE I

A ROAD OUT OF VIENNA

[It is morning in early May. Rain descends in torrents, accompanied by peals of thunder. The tepid downpour has caused the trees to assume as by magic a clothing of limp green leafage, and has turned the ruts of the uneven highway into little canals.

A drenched travelling-chariot is passing, with a meagre escort. In the interior are seated four women: the ARCHDUCHESS MARIA LOUISA, in age about eighteen; her stepmother the EMPRESS OF AUSTRIA, third wife of FRANCIS, only four years older than the ARCHDUCHESS; and two ladies of the Austrian Court. Behind come attendant carriages bearing servants and luggage.

The inmates remain for the most part silent, and appear to be in a gloomy frame of mind. From time to time they glance at the moist spring scenes which pass without in a perspective distorted by the rain-drops that slide down the panes, and by the blurring effect of the travellers' breathings. Of the four the one who keeps in the best spirits is the ARCHDUCHESS, a fair, blue-eyed, full-figured, round-lipped maiden.]

MARIA LOUISA
Whether the rain comes in or not I must open the window. Please allow me.

[She straightway opens it.]

EMPRESS [groaning]

Yes—open or shut it—I don't care. I am too ill to care for anything! [The carriage jolts into a hole.] O woe! To think that I am driven away from my husband's home in such a miserable conveyance, along such a road, and in such weather as this. [Peal of thunder.] There are his guns!

MARIA LOUISA
No, my dear one. It cannot be his guns. They told us when we started that he was only half-way from Ratisbon hither, so that he must be nearly a hundred miles off as yet; and a large army cannot move fast.

EMPRESS
He should never have been let come nearer than Ratisbon! The victory at Echmuhl was fatal for us. O Echmuhl, Echmuhl! I believe he will overtake us before we get to Buda.

FIRST LADY-IN-WAITING
If so, your Majesty, shall we be claimed as prisoners and marched to Paris?

EMPRESS
Undoubtedly. But I shouldn't much care. It would not be worse than this.... I feel sodden all through me, and frowzy, and broken!

[She closes her eyes as if to doze.]

MARIA LOUISA
It is dreadful to see her suffer so! [Shutting the window.] If the roads were not so bad I should not mind. I almost wish we had stayed; though when he arrives the cannonade will be terrible.

FIRST LADY-IN-WAITING
I wonder if he will get into Vienna. Will his men knock down all the houses, madam?

MARIA LOUISA
If he do get in, I am sure his triumph will not be for long. My uncle the Archduke Charles is at his heels! I have been told many important prophecies about Bonaparte's end, which is fast nearing, it is asserted. It is he, they say, who is referred to in the Apocalypse. He is doomed to die this year at Cologne, in an inn called "The Red Crab." I don't attach too much importance to all these predictions, but O, how glad I should be to see them come true!

SECOND LADY-IN-WAITING
So should we all, madam. What would become of his divorce-scheme then?

MARIA LOUISA
Perhaps there is nothing in that report. One can hardly believe such gossip.

SECOND LADY-IN-WAITING
But they say, your Imperial Highness, that he certainly has decided to sacrifice the Empress Josephine, and that at the meeting last October with the Emperor Alexander at Erfurt, it was even settled that he should marry as his second wife the Grand-Duchess Anne.

MARIA LOUISA

I am sure that the Empress her mother will never allow one of the house of Romanoff to marry with a bourgeois Corsican. I wouldn't if I were she!

FIRST LADY-IN-WAITING
Perhaps, your Highness, they are not so particular in Russia, where they are rather new themselves, as we in Austria, with your ancient dynasty, are in such matters.

MARIA LOUISA
Perhaps not. Though the Empress-mother is a pompous old thing, as I have been told by Prince Schwarzenberg, who was negotiating there last winter. My father says it would be a dreadful misfortune for our country if they were to marry. Though if we are to be exiled I don't see how anything of that sort can matter much.... I hope my father is safe!

[An officer of the escort rides up to the carriage window, which is opened.]

EMPRESS [unclosing her eyes]
Any more misfortunes?

OFFICER
A rumour is a-wind, your Majesty,
That the French host, the Emperor in its midst,
Lannes, Massena, and Bessieres in its van,
Advancing hither along the Ratisbon road,
Has seized the castle and town of Ebersberg,
And burnt all down, with frightful massacre,
Vast heaps of dead and wounded being consumed,
So that the streets stink strong with frizzled flesh.—
The enemy, ere this, has crossed the Traun,
Hurling brave Hiller's army back on us,
And marches on Amstetten—thirty miles
Less distant from Vienna from before!

EMPRESS
The Lord show mercy to us! But O why
Did not the Archdukes intercept the foe?

OFFICER
His Highness Archduke Charles, your Majesty,
After his sore repulse Bohemia-wards,
Could not proceed with strength and speed enough
To close in junction with the Archduke John
And Archduke Louis, as was their intent.
So Marshall Lannes swings swiftly on Vienna,
With Oudinot's and Demont's might of foot;
Then Massena and all his mounted men,
And then Napoleon, Guards, Cuirassiers,
And the main body of the Imperial Force.

EMPRESS
Alas for poor Vienna!

OFFICER
Even so!
Your Majesty has fled it none too soon.

[The window is shut, and the procession disappears behind the sheets of rain.]

SCENE II

THE ISLAND OF LOBAU, WITH WAGRAM BEYOND

[The northern horizon at the back of the bird's-eye prospect is the high ground stretching from the Bisamberg on the left to the plateau of Wagram on the right. In front of these elevations spreads the wide plain of the Marchfeld, open, treeless, and with scarcely a house upon it. (3)

In the foreground the Danube crosses the scene with a graceful slowness, looping itself round the numerous wooded islands therein. The largest of these, immediately under the eye, is the Lobau, which stands like a knot in the gnarled grain represented by the running river.

On this island can be discerned, closely packed, an enormous dark multitude of foot, horse, and artillery in French uniforms, the numbers reaching to a hundred and seventy thousand.

Lifting our eyes to discover what may be opposed to them we perceive on the Wagram plateau aforesaid, and right and left in front of it, extended lines of Austrians, whitish and glittering, to the number of a hundred and forty thousand.

The July afternoon turns to evening, the evening to twilight. A species of simmer which pervades the living spectacle raises expectation till the very air itself seems strained with suspense. A huge event of some kind is awaiting birth.]

DUMB SHOW
The first change under the cloak of night is that the tightly packed regiments on the island are got under arms. The soldiery are like a thicket of reeds in which every reed should be a man.

A large bridge connects the island with the further shore, as well as some smaller bridges. Opposite are high redoubts and ravelins that the Austrians have constructed for opposing the passage across, which the French ostentatiously set themselves to attempt by the large bridge, amid heavy cannonading.

But the movement is a feint, though this is not perceived by the Austrians as yet. The real movement is on the right hand of the foreground, behind a spur of the isle, and out of sight of the enemy; where several large rafts and flat boats, each capable of carrying three hundred men, are floated out from a screened creek.

Chosen battalions enter upon these, which immediately begin to cross with their burden. Simultaneously from other screened nooks secretly prepared floating bridges, in sections, are moved forth, joined together, and defended by those who crossed on the rafts.

At two o'clock in the morning the thousands of cooped soldiers begin to cross the bridges, producing a scene which, on such a scale, was never before witnessed in the history of war. A great discharge from the batteries accompanies this manoeuvre, arousing the Austrians to a like cannonade.

The night has been obscure for summer-time, and there is no moon. The storm now breaks in a tempestuous downpour, with lightning and thunder. The tumult of nature mingles so fantastically with the tumult of projectiles that flaming bombs and forked flashes cut the air in company, and the noise from the mortars alternates with the noise from the clouds.

From bridge to bridge and back again a gloomy-eyed figure stalks, as it has stalked the whole night long, with the restlessness of a wild animal. Plastered with mud, and dribbling with rain-water, it bears no resemblance to anything dignified or official. The figure is that of NAPOLEON, urging his multitudes over.

By daylight the great mass of the men is across the water. At six the rain ceases, the mist uncovers the face of the sun, which bristles on the helmets and bayonets of the French. A hum of amazement rises from the Austrian hosts, who turn staring faces southward and perceive what has happened, and the columns of their enemies standing to arms on the same side of the stream with themselves, and preparing to turn their left wing.

NAPOLEON rides along the front of his forces, which now spread out upon the plain, and are ranged in order of battle.

Dumb Show ends, and the point of view changes.

SCENE III

THE FIELD OF WAGRAM

[The battlefield is now viewed reversely, from the windows of a mansion at Wolkersdorf, to the rear of the Austrian position. The aspect of the windows is nearly south, and the prospect includes the plain of the Marchfeld, with the isled Danube and Lobau in the extreme distance. Ten miles to the south-west, rightwards, the faint summit of the tower of St. Stephen's, Vienna, appears. On the middle-left stands the compact plateau of Wagram, so regularly shaped as to seem as if constructed by art. On the extreme left the July sun has lately risen.

Inside the room are discovered the EMPEROR FRANCIS and some house-hold officers in attendance; with the War-Minister and Secretaries at a table at the back. Through open doors can be seen in an outer apartment adjutants, equerries, aides, and other military men. An officer in waiting enters.]

OFFICER
During the night the French have shifted, sire,

And much revised their stations of the eve
By thwart and wheeling moves upon our left,
And on our centre—projects unforeseen
Till near accomplished.

FRANCIS
But I am advised
By oral message that the Archduke Charles,
Since the sharp strife last night, has mended, too,
His earlier dispositions, and has sped
Strong orders to the Archduke John, to bring
In swiftest marches all the force he holds,
And fall with heavy impact on the French
From nigh their rear?

OFFICER
'Tis good, sire; such a swoop
Will raise an obstacle to their retreat
And refuge in the fastness of the isle;
And show this victory-gorged adventurer
That striking with a river in his rear
Is not the safest tactic to be played
Against an Austrian front equipt like ours!

[The EMPEROR FRANCIS and others scrutinize through their glasses the positions and movements of the Austrian divisions, which appear on the plain as pale masses, emitting flashes from arms and helmets under the July rays, and reaching from the Tower of Neusiedel on the left, past Wagram, into the village of Stammersdorf on the right. Beyond their lines are spread out the darker-hued French, almost parallel to the Austrians.]

FRANCIS
Those moving masses toward the right I deem
The forces of Klenau and Kollowrath,
Sent to support Prince John of Lichtenstein
I his attack that way?

[An interval.]

Now that they've gained
The right there, why is not the attack begun?

OFFICER
They are beginning on the left wing, sire.

[The EMPEROR resumes his glass and beholds bodies of men descending from the hills by Neusiedel, and crossing the Russbach river towards the French—a movement which has been going on for some time.]

FRANCIS [turning thither]

Where we are weakest! It surpasses me
To understand why was our centre thinned
To pillar up our right already strong,
Where nought is doing, while our left assault
Stands ill-supported?

[Time passes in silence.]

Yes, it is so. See,
The enemy strikes Rossenberg in flank,
Compelling him to fall behind the Russbach!

[The EMPEROR gets excited, and his face perspires. At length he cannot watch through his glass, and walks up and down.]

Penned useless here my nerves annoy my sight!
Inform me what you note.—I should opine
The Wagram height behind impregnable?

[Another silence, broken by the distant roar of the guns.]

OFFICER
Klenau and Kollowrath are pounding on!
To turn the enemy's left with our strong right
Is, after all, a plan that works out well.
Hiller and Lichtenstein conjoin therein.

FRANCIS
I hear from thence appalling cannonades.

OFFICER
'Tis their, your Majesty. Now we shall see
If the French read that there the danger lies.

FRANCIS
I only pray that Bonaparte refrain
From spying danger there till all too late!

OFFICER [involuntarily, after a pause]
Ah, Heaven!

FRANCIS [turning sharply]
Well, well? What changes figure now?

OFFICER
They pierce our centre, sire! We are, despite,
Not centrally so weak as I supposed.
Well done, Bellegarde!

FRANCIS [glancing to the centre]
And what has he well done?

OFFICER
The French in fierce fume broke through Aderklaa;
But Bellegarde, pricking along the plain behind,
Has charged and driven them back disorderly.
The Archduke Charles bounds thither, as I shape,
In person to support him!

[The EMPEROR returns to his spyglass; and they and others watch in silence, sometimes the right of their front, sometimes the centre.]

FRANCIS
It is so!
That the right attack of ours spells victory,
And Austria's grand salvation!... [Times passes.] Turn your glass,
And closely scan Napoleon and his aides
Hand-galloping towards his centre-left
To strengthen it against the brave Bellegarde.
Does your eye reach him?—That white horse, alone
In front of those that move so rapidly.

OFFICER
It does, sire; though my glass can conjure not
So cunningly as yours.... that horse must be
The famed Euphrates—him the Persian king
Sent Bonaparte as gift.

[A silence. NAPOLEON reaches a carriage that is moving across. It bears MASSENA, who, having received a recent wound, in unable to ride.]

FRANCIS
See, the white horse and horseman pause beside
A coach for some strange reason rolling there....
That white-horsed rider—yes!—is Bonaparte,
By the aides hovering round....
New war-wiles have been worded; we shall spell
Their purport soon enough! [An interval.]
The French take heart
To stand to our battalions steadfastly,
And hold their ground, having the Emperor near!

[Time passes. An aide-de-camp enters.]

AIDE
The Archduke Charles is pierced in the shoulder, sire;

He strove too far in beating back the French
At Aderklaa, and was nearly ta'en.
The wound's not serious.—On our right we win,
And deem the battle ours.

[Enter another aide-de-camp.]

SECOND AIDE
Your Majesty,
We have borne them back through Aspern village-street
And Essling is recovered. What counts more,
Their bridges to the rear we have nearly grasped,
And panic-struck they crowd the few left free,
Choking the track, with cries of "All is lost!"

FRANCIS
Then is the land delivered. God be praised!

[Exeunt aides. An interval, during which the EMPEROR and his companions again remain anxiously at
their glasses.]

There is a curious feature I discern
To have come upon the battle. On our right
We gain ground rapidly; towards the left
We lose it; and the unjudged consequence
Is that the armies; whole commingling mass
Moves like a monstrous wheel. I like it not!

[Enter another aide-de-camp.]

THIRD AIDE
Our left wing, sire, recedes before Davout,
Whom nothing can withstand! Two corps he threw
Across the Russbach up to Neusiedel,
While he himself assailed the place in front.
Of the divisions one pressed on and on,
Till lodged atop. They would have been hurled back—

FRANCIS
But how goes it with us in sum? pray say!

THIRD AIDE
We have been battered off the eastern side
Of Wagram plateau.

FRANCIS
Where's the Archduke John?
Why comes he not? One man of his here now

Were worth a host anon. And yet he tarries!

[Exit third aide. Time passes, while they reconnoitre the field with strained eyes.]

Our centre-right, it seems, round Neusiedel,
Is being repulsed! May the kind Heaven forbid
That Hesse Homberg should be yielding there!

[The Minister in attendance comes forward, and the EMPEROR consults him; then walking up and down
in silence. Another aide-de-camp enters.]

FOURTH AIDE
Sire, Neusiedel has just been wrenched from us,
And the French right is on the Wagram crest;
Nordmann has fallen, and Veczay: Hesse Homberg,
Warteachben, Muger—almost all our best—
Bleed more or less profusely!

[A gloomy silence. Exit fourth side. Ten minutes pass. Enter an officer in waiting.]

FRANCIS
What guns are those that groan from Wagram height?

OFFICER
Alas, Davout's! I have climbed the roof-top, sire,
And there discerned the truth.

[Cannonade continues. A long interval of suspense. The EMPEROR returns to his glass.]

FRANCIS
A part of it!
There seems to be a grim, concerted lunge
By the whole strength of France upon our right,
Centre, and left wing simultaneously!

OFFICER
Most viciously upon the centre, sire,
If I mistook not, hard by Sussenbrunn;
The assault is led by Bonaparte in person,
Who shows himself with marvellous recklessness,
Yet like a phantom-fiend receives no hurt.

FRANCIS [still gazing]
Ha! Now the Archduke Charles has seen the intent,
And taken steps against it. Sussenbrunn
Must be the threatened thing. [Silence.] What an advance!—
Straight hitherward. Our centre girdles them.—
Surely they'll not persist? Who heads that charge?

OFFICER
They say Macdonald, sire.

FRANCIS
Meagrest remains
Will there be soon of those in that advance!
We are burning them to bones by our hot fire.
They are almost circumscribed: if fully so
The battle's ours! What's that behind them, eh?

OFFICER
Their last reserves, that they may feed the front,
And sterilize our hope!

FRANCIS
Yes, their reserve—
Dragoons and cuirassiers—charge in support.
You see their metal gleaming as they come.
Well, it is neck or nothing for them now!

OFFICER
It's nothing, sire. Their charge of cavalry
Has desperately failed.

FRANCIS
Their foot press on,
However, with a battery in front
Which deals the foulest damage done us yet. [Time passes.]
They ARE effecting lodgment, after all.
Who would have reckoned on't—our men so firm!

[Re-enter first aide-de-camp.]

FIRST AIDE
The Archduke Charles retreats, your majesty;
And the issue wears a dirty look just now.

FRANCIS [gloomily]
Yes: I have seen the signs for some good while.
But he retreats with blows, and orderly.

[Time passes, till the sun has rounded far towards the west. The features of the battle now materially
change. The French have regained Aspern and Essling; the Austrian army is doubled back from the
Danube and from the heights of Wagram, which, as viewed from Wolkersdorf, face the afternoon shine,
the French established thereon glittering in the rays.

FRANCIS [choking a sigh]

The turn has passed. We are worsted, but not overwhelmed!...
The French advance is laboured, and but slow.
—This might have been another-coloured day
If but the Archduke John had joined up promptly;
Yet still he lags!

ANOTHER OFFICER [lately entered]
He's just now coming, sire.
His columns glimmer in the Frenchmen's rear.
Past Siebenbrunn's and Loebensdorf's smoked hills.
FRANCIS [impatiently]

Ay—coming NOW! Why could he not be COME!

[They watch intently.]

We can see nothing of that side from here.

[Enter a general officer, who speaks to the Minister at the back of the room.]

MINISTER [coming forward]
Your Majesty, I now have to suggest,
Pursuant to conclusions reached this morn,
That since the front and flower of all our force
Is seen receding to the Bisamberg,
These walls no longer yield safe shade for you,
Or facile outlook. Scouts returning say
Either Davout, or Bonaparte himself,
With the mid-columns of his forward corps,
Will bear up hitherward in fierce pursuit,
And may intrude beneath this very roof.
Not yet, I think; it may not be to-night;
But we should stand prepared.

FRANCIS
If we must go
We'll go with a good grace, unfeignedly!
Who knows to-morrow may not see regained
What we have lost to-day?

[Re-enter fourth aide-de-camp.]

FOURTH AIDE [breathlessly]
The Archduke John,
Discerning our main musters in retreat,
Abandons an advance that throws on him
The enemy's whole brunt if he bear on.

FRANCIS
Alas for his devotion! Let us go.
Such weight of sadness as we shoulder now
Will wring us down to sleep in stall or stye,
If even that be found!... Think! Bonaparte,
By reckless riskings of his life and limb,
Has turned the steelyard of our strength to-day
Whilst I have idled here!... May brighter times
Attend the cause of Europe far in Spain,
And British blood flow not, as ours, in vain!

[Exeunt the EMPEROR FRANCIS, minister, officers, and attendants. The night comes, and the scene is obscured.]

SCENE IV

THE FIELD OF TALAVERA

[It is the same month and weather as in the preceding scene.

Talavera town, on the river Tagus, is at the extreme right of the foreground; a mountain range on the extreme left.

The allied army under SIR ARTHUR WELLESLEY stretches between—the English on the left, the Spanish on the right—part holding a hill to the left-centre of the scene, divided from the mountains by a valley, and part holding a redoubt to the right-centre. This army of more than fifty thousand all told, of which twenty-two thousand only are English, has its back to the spectator.

Beyond, in a wood of olive, oak, and cork, are the fifty to sixty thousand French, facing the spectator and the allies. Their right includes a strong battery upon a hill which fronts the one on the English left.

Behind all, the heights of Salinas close the prospect, the small river Alberche flowing at their foot from left to right into the Tagus, which advances in foreshortened perspective to the town at the right front corner of the scene as aforesaid.]

DUMB SHOW
The hot and dusty July afternoon having turned to twilight, shady masses of men start into motion from the French position, come towards the foreground, silently ascend the hill on the left of the English, and assail the latter in a violent outburst of fire and lead. They nearly gain possession of the hill ascended.

CHORUS OF RUMOURS [aerial music]
Talavera tongues it as ten o' the night-time:
Now come Ruffin's slaughterers surging upward,
Backed by bold Vilatte's! From the vale Lapisse, too,
Darkly outswells there!

Down the vague veiled incline the English fling them,
Bended bayonets prodding opponents backward:
So the first fierce charge of the ardent Frenchmen
England repels there!

Having fallen back into the darkness the French presently re-ascend in yet larger masses. The high square knapsack which every English foot-soldier carries, and his shako, and its tuft, outline themselves against the dim light as the ranks stand awaiting the shock.

CHORUS OF RUMOURS
Pushing spread they!—shout as they reach the summit!—
Strength and stir new-primed in their plump battalions:
Puffs of barbed flame blown on the lines opposing
Higher and higher.

There those hold them mute, though at speaking distance—
Mute, while clicking flints, and the crash of volleys
Whelm the weighted gloom with immense distraction
Pending their fire.

Fronting heads, helms, brows can each ranksman read there,
Epaulettes, hot cheeks, and the shining eyeball,
[Called a trice from gloom by the fleeting pan-flash]
Pressing them nigher!
The French again fall back in disorder into the hollow, and LAPISSE draws off on the right. As the sinking sound of the muskets tells what has happened the English raise a shout.

CHORUS OF PITIES
Thus the dim nocturnal embroil of conflict
Closes with the roar of receding gun-fire.
Harness loosened then, and their day-long strenuous
Temper unbending,

Worn-out lines lie down where they late stood staunchly—
Cloaks around them rolled—by the bivouac embers:
There at dawn to stake in the dynasts' death-game
All, till the ending!

SCENE V

THE SAME

DUMB SHOW [continued]
The morning breaks. There is another murderous attempt to dislodge the English from the hill, the assault being pressed with a determination that excites the admiration of the English themselves.

The French are seen descending into the valley, crossing it, and climbing it on the English side under the fire of HILL'S whole division, all to no purpose. In their retreat they leave behind them on the slopes nearly two thousand lying.

The day advances to noon, and the air trembles in the intense heat. The combat flags, and is suspended.

SPIRIT OF THE PITIES
What do I see but thirsty, throbbing bands
From these inimic hosts defiling down
In homely need towards the little stream
That parts their enmities, and drinking there!
They get to grasping hands across the rill,
Sealing their sameness as earth's sojourners.—
What more could plead the wryness of the time
Than such unstudied piteous pantomimes!

SPIRIT IRONIC
It is only that Life's queer mechanics chance to work out in this grotesque shape just now. The groping tentativeness of an Immanent Will [as grey old Years describes it] cannot be asked to learn logic at this time of day! The spectacle of Its instruments, set to riddle one another through, and then to drink together in peace and concord, is where the humour comes in, and makes the play worth seeing!

SPIRIT SINISTER
Come, Sprite, don't carry your ironies too far, or you may wake up the Unconscious Itself, and tempt It to let all the gory clock-work of the show run down to spite me!

DUMB SHOW [continuing]
The drums roll, and the men of the two nations part from their comradeship at the Alberche brook, the dark masses of the French army assembling anew. SIR ARTHUR WELLESLEY has seated himself on a mound that commands a full view of the contested hill, and remains there motionless a long time. When the French form for battle he is seen to have come to a conclusion. He mounts, gives his orders, and the aides ride off.

The French advance steadily through the sultry atmosphere, the skirmishers in front, and the columns after, moving, yet seemingly motionless. Their eighty cannon peal out and their shots mow every space in the line of them. Up the great valley and the terraces of the hill whose fame is at that moment being woven, comes VILLATE, boring his way with foot and horse, and RUFFIN'S men following behind.

According to the order given, the Twenty-third Light Dragoons and the German Hussars advance at a chosen moment against the head of these columns. On the way they disappear.

SPIRIT OF THE PITIES
Why this bedevilment? What can have chanced?

SPIRIT OF RUMOUR
It so befalls that as their chargers near
The inimical wall of flesh with its iron frise,
A treacherous chasm uptrips them: zealous men

And docile horses roll to dismal death
And horrid mutilation.

SPIRIT OF THE PITIES
Those who live
Even now advance! I'll see no more. Relate.

SPIRIT OF RUMOUR
Yes, those pant on. Then further Frenchmen cross,
And Polish Lancers, and Westphalian Horse,
Who ring around these luckless Islanders,
And sweep them down like reeds by the river-bank
In scouring floods; till scarce a man remains.

Meanwhile on the British right SEBASTIANI'S corps has precipitated itself in column against GENERAL
CAMPBELL'S division, the division of LAPISSE against the centre, and at the same time the hill on the
English left is again assaulted. The English and their allies are pressed sorely here, the bellowing battery
tearing lanes through their masses.

SPIRIT OF RUMOUR [continuing]
The French reserves of foot and horse now on,
Smiting the Islanders in breast and brain
Till their mid-lines are shattered.... Now there ticks
The moment of the crisis; now the next,
Which brings the turning stroke.

SIR ARTHUR WELLESLEY sends down the Forty-eighth regiment under COLONEL DONELLAN to support
the wasting troops. It advances amid those retreating, opening to let them pass.

SPIRIT OF THE RUMOUR [continuing]
The pales, enerved,
The hitherto unflinching enemy!
Lapisse is pierced to death; the flagging French
Decline into the hollows whence they came.
The too exhausted English and reduced
Lack strength to follow.—Now the western sun,
Conning with unmoved visage quick and dead,
Gilds horsemen slackening, and footmen stilled,
Till all around breathes drowsed hostility.

Last, the swealed herbage lifts a leering light,
And flames traverse the field; and hurt and slain
Opposed, opposers, in a common plight
Are scorched together on the dusk champaign.
The fire dies down, and darkness enwraps the scene.

SCENE VI

BRIGHTON. THE ROYAL PAVILION

[It is the birthday dinner-party of the PRINCE OF WALES. In the floridly decorated banqueting-room stretch tables spread with gold and silver plate, and having artificial fountains in their midst.

Seated at the tables are the PRINCE himself as host—rosy, well curled, and affable—the DUKES OF YORK, CLARENCE, KENT, SUSSEX, CUMBERLAND, and CAMBRIDGE, with many noblemen, including LORDS HEADFORT, BERKELEY, EGREMONT, CHICHESTER, DUDLEY, SAY AND SELE, SOUTHAMPTON, HEATHFIELD, ERSKINE, KEITH, C. SOMERSET, G. CAVENDISH, R. SEYMOUR, and others; SIR C. POLE, SIR E.G. DE CRESPIGNY, MR. SHERIDAN; Generals, Colonels, and Admirals, and the REV. MR. SCOTT.

The PRINCE'S band plays in the adjoining room. The banquet is drawing to its close, and a boisterous conversation is in progress.

Enter COLONEL BLOOMFIELD with a dispatch for the PRINCE, who looks it over amid great excitement in the company. In a few moments silence is called.]

PRINCE OF WALES
I have the joy, my lords and gentlemen,
To rouse you with the just imported tidings
From General Wellesley through Lord Castlereagh
Of a vast victory [noisy cheers] over the French in Spain.
The place—called Talavera de la Reyna
[If I pronounce it rightly]—long unknown,
Wears not the crest and blazonry of fame! [Cheers.]
The heads and chief contents of the dispatch
I read you as succinctly as I can. [Cheers.]

SHERIDAN [singing sotto voce]
"Now foreign foemen die and fly,
Dammy, we'll drink little England dry!"

[The PRINCE reads the parts of the dispatch that describe the battle, amid intermittent cheers.]

PRINCE OF WALES [continuing]
Such is the substance of the news received,
Which, after Wagram, strikes us genially
As sudden sunrise through befogged night shades!

SHERIDAN [privately]
By God, that's good, sir! You are a poet born, while the rest of us
are but made, and bad at that.

[The health of the army in Spain is drunk with acclamations.]

PRINCE OF WALES [continuing]

In this achievement we, alas! have lost
Too many! Yet such blanks must ever be.—
Mackenzie, Langworth, Beckett of the Guards,
Have fallen of ours; while of the enemy
Generals Lapisse and Morlot are laid low.—
Drink to their memories!

[They drink in silence.]

Other news, my friends,
Received to-day is of like hopeful kind.
The Great War-Expedition to the Scheldt [Cheers.]
Which lately sailed, has found a favouring wind,
And by this hour has touched its destined shores.
The enterprise will soon be hot aglow,
The invaders making first the Cadsand coast,
And then descending on Walcheren Isle.
But items of the next step are withheld
Till later days, from obvious policy. [Cheers.]

[Faint throbbing sounds, like the notes of violincellos and contrabassos, reach the ear from some building without as the speaker pauses.

In worthy emulation of us here
The county holds to-night a birthday ball,
Which flames with all the fashion of the town.
I have been asked to patronize their revel,
And sup with them, and likewise you, my guests.
We have good reason, with such news to hear!
Thither we haste and join our loyal friends,
And stir them with this live intelligence
Of our staunch regiments on the Spanish plains. [Applause.]
With them we'll now knit hands and beat the ground,
And bring in dawn as we whirl round and round!
There are some fair ones in their set to-night,
And such we need here in our bachelor-plight. [Applause.]

[The PRINCE, his brothers, and a large proportion of the other Pavilion guests, swagger out in the direction of the Castle assembly-rooms adjoining, and the deserted banqueting-hall grows dark. In a few moments the back of the scene opens, revealing the assembly-rooms behind.]

SCENE VII

THE SAME. THE ASSEMBLY ROOMS

[The rooms are lighted with candles in brass chandeliers, and a dance is in full movement to the strains of a string-band. A signal is given, shortly after the clock has struck eleven, by MR. FORTH, Master of Ceremonies.]

FORTH
His Royal Highness comes, though somewhat late,
But never too late for welcome! [Applause.] Dancers, stand,
That we may do fit homage to the Prince
Who soon may shine our country's gracious king.

[After a brief stillness a commotion is heard at the door, the band strikes up the National air, and the PRINCE enters, accompanied by the rest of the visitors from the Pavilion. The guests who have been temporarily absent now crowd in, till there is hardly space to stand.]

PRINCE OF WALES [wiping his face and whispering to Sheridan]
What shall I say to fit their feeling here?
Damn me, that other speech has stumped me quite!

SHERIDAN [whispering]
If heat be evidence of loy—

PRINCE OF WALES
If what?

SHERIDAN
If heat be evidence of loyalty,
Et caetera—something quaint like that might please 'em.

PRINCE OF WALES [to the company]
If heat be evidence of loyalty,
This room affords it truly without question;
If heat be not, then its accompaniment
Most surely 'tis to-night. The news I bring,
Good ladies, friends, and gentlemen, perchance
You have divined already? That our arms—
Engaged to thwart Napoleon's tyranny
Over the jaunty, jocund land of Spain
Even to the highest apex of our strength—
Are rayed with victory! [Cheers.] Lengthy was the strife
And fierce, and hot; and sore the suffering;
But proudly we endured it; and shall hear,
No doubt, of its far consequence
Ere many days. I'll read the details sent.

[Cheers.]

[He reads again from the dispatch amid more cheering, the ball-room guests crowding round. When he has done he answers questions; then continuing:

Meanwhile our interest is, if possible,
As keenly waked elsewhere. Into the Scheldt
Some forty thousand bayonets and swords,
And twoscore ships o' the line, with frigates, sloops,
And gunboats sixty more, make headway now,
Bleaching the waters with their bellying sails;
Or maybe they already anchor there,
And that level ooze of Walcheren shore
Ring with the voices of that landing host
In every twang of British dialect,
Clamorous to loosen fettered Europe's chain!

[Cheers.]

A NOBLE LORD [aside to Sheridan]
Prinny's outpouring tastes suspiciously like your brew, Sheridan. I'll be damned if it is his own
concoction. How d'ye sell it a gallon?

SHERIDAN
I don't deal that way nowadays. I give the recipe, and charge a duty on the gauging. It is more artistic,
and saves trouble.

[The company proceed to the supper-rooms, and the ball-room sinks into solitude.]

SPIRIT OF THE PITIES
So they pass on. Let be!—But what is this—
A moan?—all frailly floating from the east
To usward, even from the forenamed isle?...
Would I had not broke nescience, to inspect
A world so ill-contrived!

SPIRIT OF THE YEARS
But since thou hast
We'll hasten to the isle; and thou'lt behold—
Such as it is—the scene its coasts enfold.

SCENE VIII

WALCHEREN

[A marshy island at the mouth of the Scheldt, lit by the low sunshine of an evening in late summer. The
horizontal rays from the west lie in yellow sheaves across the vapours that the day's heat has drawn
from the sweating soil. Sour grasses grow in places, and strange fishy smells, now warm, now cold, pass
along. Brass-hued and opalescent bubbles, compounded of many gases, rise where passing feet have
trodden the damper spots. At night the place is the haunt of the Jack-lantern.]

DUMB SHOW
A vast army is encamped here, and in the open spaces are infantry on parade—skeletoned men, some flushed, some shivering, who are kept moving because it is dangerous to stay still. Every now and then one falls down, and is carried away to a hospital with no roof, where he is laid, bedless, on the ground.

In the distance soldiers are digging graves for the funerals which are to take place after dark, delayed till then that the sight of so many may not drive the living melancholy-mad. Faint noises are heard in the air.

SHADE OF THE EARTH
What storm is this of souls dissolved in sighs,
And what the dingy doom it signifies?

SPIRIT OF THE PITIES
We catch a lamentation shaped thuswise:

CHORUS OF THE PITIES [aerial music]
"We who withstood the blasting blaze of war
When marshalled by the gallant Moore awhile,
Beheld the grazing death-bolt with a smile,
Closed combat edge to edge and bore to bore,
Now rot upon this Isle!

"The ever wan morass, the dune, the blear
Sandweed, and tepid pool, and putrid smell,
Emaciate purpose to a fractious fear,
Beckon the body to its last low cell—
A chink no chart will tell.

"O ancient Delta, where the fen-lights flit!
Ignoble sediment of loftier lands,
Thy humour clings about our hearts and hands
And solves us to its softness, till we sit
As we were part of it.

"Such force as fever leaves maddened now,
With tidings trickling in from day to day
Of others' differing fortunes, wording how
They yield their lives to baulk a tyrant's sway—
Yield them not vainly, they!

"In champaigns green and purple, far and near,
In town and thorpe where quiet spire-cocks turn,
Through vales, by rocks, beside the brooding burn
Echoes the aggressor's arrogant career;
And we pent pithless here!

"Here, where each creeping day the creeping file
Draws past with shouldered comrades score on score,
Bearing them to their lightless last asile,
Where weary wave-wails from the clammy shore
Will reach their ears no more.

"We might have fought, and had we died, died well,
Even if in dynasts' discords not our own;
Our death-spot some sad haunter might have shown,
Some tongue have asked our sires or sons to tell
The tale of how we fell;

"But such be chanced not. Like the mist we fade,
No lustrous lines engrave in story we,
Our country's chiefs, for their own fames afraid,
Will leave our names and fates by this pale sea,
To perish silently!"

SPIRIT OF THE YEARS
Why must ye echo as mechanic mimes
These mortal minion's bootless cadences,
Played on the stops of their anatomy
As is the mewling music on the strings
Of yonder ship-masts by the unweeting wind,
Or the frail tune upon this withering sedge
That holds its papery blades against the gale?
—Men pass to dark corruption, at the best,
Ere I can count five score: these why not now?—
The Immanent Shaper builds Its beings so
Whether ye sigh their sighs with them or no!
The night fog enwraps the isle and the dying English army.

ACT FIFTH

SCENE I

PARIS. A BALLROOM IN THE HOUSE OF CAMBACERES

[The many-candled saloon at the ARCH-CHANCELLOR'S is visible through a draped opening, and a crowd of masked dancers in fantastic costumes revolve, sway, and intermingle to the music that proceeds from an alcove at the further end of the same apartment. The front of the scene is a withdrawing-room of smaller size, now vacant, save for the presence of one somber figure, that of NAPOLEON, seated and apparently watching the moving masquerade.]

SPIRIT OF THE PITIES

Napoleon even now embraces not
From stress of state affairs, which hold him grave
Through revels that might win the King of Spleen
To toe a measure! I would speak with him.

SPIRIT OF THE YEARS
Speak if thou wilt whose speech nor mars nor mends!

SPIRIT OF THE PITIES [into Napoleon's ear]
Why thus and thus Napoleon? Can it be
That Wagram with its glories, shocks, and shames,
Still leaves athirst the palate of thy pride?

NAPOLEON [answering as in soliloquy]
The trustless, timorous lease of human life
Warns me to hedge in my diplomacy.
The sooner, then, the safer! Ay, this eve,
This very night, will I take steps to rid
My morrows of the weird contingencies
That vision round and make one hollow-eyed....
The unexpected, lurid death of Lannes—
Rigid as iron, reaped down like a straw—
Tiptoed Assassination haunting round
In unthought thoroughfares, the near success
Of Staps the madman, argue to forbid
The riskful blood of my previsioned line
And potence for dynastic empery
To linger vialled in my veins alone.
Perhaps within this very house and hour,
Under an innocent mask of Love or Hope,
Some enemy queues my ways to coffin me....
When at the first clash of the late campaign,
A bold belief in Austria's star prevailed,
There pulsed quick pants of expectation round
Among the cowering kings, that too well told
What would have fared had I been overthrown!
So; I must send down shoots to future time
Who'll plant my standard and my story there;
And a way opens.—Better I had not
Bespoke a wife from Alexander's house.
Not there now lies my look. But done is done!

[The dance ends and masks enter, BERTHIER among them. NAPOLEON beckons to him, and he comes
forward.]

God send you find amid this motley crew
Frivolities enough, friend Berthier—eh?
My thoughts have worn oppressive shades despite such!

What scandals of me do they bandy here?
These close disguises render women bold—
Their shames being of the light, not of the thing—
And your sagacity has garnered much,
I make no doubt, of ill and good report,
That marked our absence from the capital?

BERTHIER
Methinks, your Majesty, the enormous tale
Of your campaign, like Aaron's serpent-rod,
Has swallowed up the smaller of its kind.
Some speak, 'tis true, in counterpoise thereto,
Of English deeds by Talavera town,
Though blurred by their exploit at Walcheren,
And all its crazy, crass futilities.

NAPOLEON
Yet was the exploit well featured in design,
Large in idea, and imaginative;
I had not deemed the blinkered English folk
So capable of view. Their fate contrived
To place an idiot at the helm of it,
Who marred its working, else it had been hard
If things had not gone seriously for us.
—But see, a lady saunters hitherward
Whose gait proclaims her Madame Metternich,
One that I fain would speak with.

[NAPOLEON rises and crosses the room toward a lady-masker who has just appeared in the opening.
BERTHIER draws off, and the EMPEROR, unceremoniously taking the lady's arm, brings her forward to a
chair, and sits down beside her as dancing is resumed.]

MADAME METTERNICH
In a flash
I recognized you, sire; as who would not
The bearer of such deep-delved charactery?

NAPOLEON
The devil, madame, take your piercing eyes!
It's hard I cannot prosper in a game
That every coxcomb plays successfully.
—So here you are still, though your loving lord
Disports him at Vienna?

MADAME METTERNICH
Paris, true,
Still holds me; though in quiet, save to-night,
When I have been expressly prayed come hither,

Or I had not left home.

NAPOLEON
I sped that Prayer!—
I have a wish to put a case to you,
Wherein a woman's judgment, such as yours,
May be of signal service. [He lapses into reverie.]

MADAME METTERNICH
Well? The case—

NAPOLEON
Is marriage—mine.

MADAME METTERNICH
It is beyond me, sire!

NAPOLEON
You glean that I have decided to dissolve
[Pursuant to monitions murmured long]
My union with the present Empress—formed
Without the Church's due authority?

MADAME METTERNICH
Vaguely. And that light tentatives have winged
Betwixt your Majesty and Russia's court,
To moot that one of their Grand Duchesses
Should be your Empress-wife. Nought else I know.

NAPOLEON
There have been such approachings; more, worse luck.
Last week Champagny wrote to Alexander
Asking him for his sister—yes or no.

MADAME METTERNICH
What "worse luck" lies in that, your Majesty,
If severance from the Empress Josephine
Be fixed unalterably?

NAPOLEON
This worse luck lies there:
If your Archduchess, Marie Louise the fair,
Would straight accept my hand, I'd offer it,
And throw the other over. Faith, the Tsar
Has shown such backwardness in answering me,
Time meanwhile trotting, that I have ample ground
For such withdrawal.—Madame, now, again,
Will your Archduchess marry me of no?

MADAME METTERNICH
Your sudden questions quite confound my sense!
It is impossible to answer them.

NAPOLEON
Well, madame, now I'll put it to you thus:
Were you in the Archduchess Marie's place
Would you accept my hand—and heart therewith?

MADAME METTERNICH
I should refuse you—most assuredly! (4)

NAPOLEON [laughing roughly]
Ha-ha! That's frank. And devilish cruel too!
—Well, write to your husband. Ask him what he thinks,
And let me know.

MADAME METTERNICH
Indeed, sire, why should I?
There goes the Ambassador, Prince Schwarzenberg,
Successor to my spouse. He's now the groove
And proper conduit of diplomacy
Through whom to broach this matter to his Court.

NAPOLEON
Do you, then, broach it through him, madame, pray;
Now, here, to-night.

MADAME METTERNICH
I will, informally,
To humour you, on this recognizance,
That you leave not the business in my hands,
But clothe your project in official guise
Through him to-morrow; so safeguarding me
From foolish seeming, as the babbler forth
Of a fantastic and unheard of dream.

NAPOLEON
I'll send Eugene to him, as you suggest.
Meanwhile prepare him. Make your stand-point this:
Children are needful to my dynasty,
And if one woman cannot mould them for me,
Why, then, another must.

[Exit NAPOLEON abruptly. Dancing continues. MADAME METTERNICH sits on, musing. Enter
SCHWARZENBERG.]

MADAME METTERNICH
The Emperor has just left me. We have tapped
This theme and that; his empress and—his next.
Ay, so! Now, guess you anything?

SCHWARZENBERG
Of her?
No more than that the stock of Romanoff
Will not supply the spruce commodity.

MADAME METTERNICH
And that the would-be customer turns toe
To our shop in Vienna.

SCHWARZENBERG
Marvellous;
And comprehensible but as the dream
Of Delaborde, of which I have lately heard.
It will not work!—What think you, madame, on't?

MADAME METTERNICH
That it will work, and is as good as wrought!—
I break it to you thus, at his request.
In brief time Prince Eugene will wait on you,
And make the formal offer in his name.

SCHWARZENBERG
Which I can but receive ad referendum,
And shall initially make clear as much,
Disclosing not a glimpse of my own mind!
Meanwhile you make good Metternich aware?

MADAME METTERNICH
I write this midnight, that amaze may pitch
To coolness ere your messenger arrives.

SCHWARZENBERG
This radiant revelation flicks a gleam
On many circling things!—the courtesies
Which graced his bearing toward our officer
Amid the tumults of the late campaign,
His wish for peace with England, his affront
At Alexander's tedious-timed reply...
Well, it will thrust a thorn in Russia's side,
If I err not, whatever else betide!

[Exeunt. The maskers surge into the foreground of the scene, and their motions become more and more fantastic. A strange gloom begins and intensifies, until only the high lights of their grinning figures are visible. These also, with the whole ball-room, gradually darken, and the music softens to silence.]

[The evening of the next day. A saloon of the Palace, with folding-doors communicating with a dining-room. The doors are flung open, revealing on the dining-table an untouched dinner, NAPOLEON and JOSEPHINE rising from it, and DE BAUSSET, chamberlain-in-waiting, pacing up and down. The EMPEROR and EMPRESS come forward into the saloon, the latter pale and distressed, and patting her eyes with her handkerchief.

The doors are closed behind them; a page brings in coffee; NAPOLEON signals to him to leave. JOSEPHINE goes to pour out the coffee, but NAPOLEON pushes her aside and pours it out himself, looking at her in a way which causes her to sink cowering into a chair like a frightened animal.]

JOSEPHINE
I see my doom, my friend, upon your face!

NAPOLEON
You see me bored by Cambaceres' ball.

JOSEPHINE
It means divorce!—a thing more terrible
Than carrying elsewhere the dalliances
That formerly were mine. I kicked at that;
But now agree, as I for long have done,
To any infidelities of act
May I be yours in name!

NAPOLEON
My mind must bend
To other things than our domestic petting:
The Empire orbs above our happiness,
And 'tis the Empire dictates this divorce.
I reckon on your courage and calm sense
To breast with me the law's formalities,
And get it through before the year has flown.

JOSEPHINE
But are you REALLY going to part from me?
O no, no, my dear husband; no, in truth,
It cannot be my Love will serve me so!

NAPOLEON
I mean but mere divorcement, as I said,
On simple grounds of sapient sovereignty.

JOSEPHINE
But nothing have I done save good to you:—
Since the fond day we wedded into one
I never even have THOUGHT you jot of harm!
Many the happy junctures when you have said
I stood as guardian-angel over you,
As your Dame Fortune, too, and endless things
Of such-like pretty tenour—yes, you have!
Then how can you so gird against me now?
You had not pricked upon it much of late,
And so I hoped and hoped the ugly spectre
Had been laid dead and still.

NAPOLEON [impatiently]
I tell you, dear,
The thing's decreed, and even the princess chosen.

JOSEPHINE
Ah—so—the princess chosen!... I surmise
It is none else than the Grand-Duchess Anne:
Gossip was right—though I would not believe.
She's young; but no great beauty!—Yes, I see
Her silly, soulless eyes and horrid hair;
In which new gauderies you'll forget sad me!

NAPOLEON
Upon my soul you are childish, Josephine:
A woman of your years to pout it so!—
I say it's not the Tsar's Grand-Duchess Anne.

JOSEPHINE
Some other Fair, then. You whose name can nod
The flower of all the world's virginity
Into your bed, will well take care of that!
[Spitefully.] She may not have a child, friend, after all.

NAPOLEON [drily]
You hope she won't, I know!—But don't forget
Madame Walewska did, and had she shown
Such cleverness as yours, poor little fool,
Her withered husband might have been displaced,
And her boy made my heir.—Well, let that be.
The severing parchments will be signed by us
Upon the fifteenth, prompt.

JOSEPHINE
What—I have to sign
My putting away upon the fifteenth next?

NAPOLEON
Ay—both of us.

JOSEPHINE [falling on her knees]
So far advanced—so far!
Fixed?—for the fifteenth? O I do implore you,
My very dear one, by our old, old love,
By my devotion, don't cast me off
Now, after these long years!

NAPOLEON
Heavens, how you jade me!
Must I repeat that I don't cast you off;
We merely formally arrange divorce—
We live and love, but call ourselves divided.

[A silence.]

JOSEPHINE [with sudden calm]
Very well. Let it be. I must submit! [Rises.]

NAPOLEON
And this much likewise you must promise me,
To act in the formalities thereof
As if you shaped them of your own free will.

JOSEPHINE
How can I—when no freewill's left in me?

NAPOLEON
You are a willing party—do you hear?

JOSEPHINE [quivering]
I hardly—can—bear this!—It is—too much
For a poor weak and broken woman's strength!
But—but I yield!—I am so helpless now:
I give up all—ay, kill me if you will,
I won't cry out!

NAPOLEON
And one thing further still,
You'll help me in my marriage overtures
To win the Duchess—Austrian Marie she,—

Concentrating all your force to forward them.

JOSEPHINE
It is the—last humiliating blow!—
I cannot—O, I will not!

NAPOLEON [fiercely]
But you SHALL!
And from your past experience you may know
That what I say I mean!

JOSEPHINE [breaking into sobs]
O my dear husband—do not make me—don't!
If you but cared for me—the hundredth part
Of how—I care for you, you could not be
So cruel as to lay this torture on me.
It hurts me so!—it cuts me like a sword.
Don't make me, dear! Don't, will you! O,O,O!

[She sinks down in a hysterical fit.]

NAPOLEON [calling]
Bausset!

[Enter DE BAUSSET, Chamberlain-in-waiting.]

Bausset, come in and shut the door.
Assist me here. The Empress has fallen ill.
Don't call for help. We two can carry her
By the small private staircase to her rooms.
Here—I will take her feet.

[They lift JOSEPHINE between them and carry her out. Her moans die away as they recede towards the stairs. Enter two servants, who remove coffee-service, readjust chairs, etc.]

FIRST SERVANT
So, poor old girl, she's wailed her Missere Mei, as Mother Church says. I knew she was to get the sack ever since he came back.

SECOND SERVANT
Well, there will be a little civil huzzaing, a little crowing and cackling among the Bonapartes at the downfall of the Beauharnais family at last, mark me there will! They've had their little hour, as the poets say, and now 'twill be somebody else's turn. O it is droll! Well, Father Time is a great philosopher, if you take him right. Who is to be the new woman?

FIRST SERVANT
She that contains in her own corporation the necessary particular.

SECOND SERVANT
And what may they be?

FIRST SERVANT
She must be young.

SECOND SERVANT
Good. She must. The country must see to that.

FIRST SERVANT
And she must be strong.

SECOND SERVANT
Good again. She must be strong. The doctors will see to that.

FIRST SERVANT
And she must be fruitful as the vine.

SECOND SERVANT
Ay, by God. She must be fruitful as the vine. That, Heaven help him, he must see to himself, like the meanest multiplying man in Paris.

[Exeunt servant. Re-enter NAPOLEON with his stepdaughter, Queen Hortense.]

NAPOLEON
Your mother is too rash and reasonless—
Wailing and fainting over statesmanship
Which is no personal caprice of mine,
But policy most painful—forced on me
By the necessities of this country's charge.
Go to her; see if she be saner now;
Explain it to her once and once again,
And bring me word what impress you may make.

[HORTENSE goes out. CHAMPAGNY is shown in.]

Champagny, I have something clear to say
Now, on our process after the divorce.
The question of the Russian Duchess Anne
Was quite inept for further toying with.
The years rush on, and I grow nothing younger.
So I have made up my mind—committed me
To Austria and the Hapsburgs—good or ill!
It was the best, most practicable plunge,
And I have plunged it.

CHAMPAGNY
Austria say you, sire?

I reckoned that but a scurrying dream!

NAPOLEON
Well, so it was. But such a pretty dream
That its own charm transfixed it to a notion,
That showed itself in time a sanity,
Which hardened in its turn to a resolve
As firm as any built by mortal mind.—
The Emperor's consent must needs be won;
But I foresee no difficulty there.
The young Archduchess is a bright blond thing
By general story; and considering, too,
That her good mother childed seventeen times,
It will be hard if she can not produce
The modest one or two that I require.

[Enter DE BAUSSET with dispatches.]

DE BAUSSET
The courier, sire, from Petersburg is here,
And brings these letters for your Majesty.

[Exit DE BAUSSET.]

NAPOLEON [after silently reading]

Ha-ha! It never rains unless it pours:
Now I can have the other readily.
The proverb hits me aptly: "Well they do
Who doff the old love ere they don the new!"
[He glances again over the letter.]
Yes, Caulaincourt now writes he has every hope
Of quick success in settling the alliance!
The Tsar is willing—even anxious for it,
His sister's youth the single obstacle.
The Empress-mother, hitherto against me,
Ambition-fired, verges on suave consent,
Likewise the whole Imperial family.
What irony is all this to me now!
Time lately was when I had leapt thereat.

CHAMPAGNY
You might, of course, sire, give th' Archduchess up,
Seeing she looms uncertainly as yet,
While this does so no longer.

NAPOLEON
No—not I.

My sense of my own dignity forbids
My watching the slow clocks of Muscovy!
Why have they dallied with my tentatives
In pompous silence since the Erfurt day?
—And Austria, too, affords a safer hope.
The young Archduchess is much less a child
Than is the other, who, Caulaincourt says,
Will be incapable of motherhood
For six months yet or more—a grave delay.

CHAMPAGNY
Your Majesty appears to have trimmed your sail
For Austria; and no more is to be said!

NAPOLEON
Except that there's the house of Saxony
If Austria fail.—then, very well, Champagny,
Write you to Caulaincourt accordingly.

CHAMPAGNY
I will, your Majesty.

[Exit CHAMPAGNY. Re-enter QUEEN HORTENSE.]

NAPOLEON
Ah, dear Hortense,
How is your mother now?

HORTENSE
Calm, quite calm, sire.
I pledge me you need have no further fret
From her entreating tears. She bids me say
That now, as always, she submits herself
With chastened dignity to circumstance,
And will descend, at notice, from your throne—
As in days earlier she ascended it—
In questionless obedience to your will.
It was your hand that crowned her; let it be
Likewise your hand that takes her crown away.
As for her children, we shall be but glad
To follow and withdraw ourselves with her,
The tenderest mother children ever knew,
From grandeurs that have brought no happiness!

NAPOLEON [taking her hand]
But, Hortense, dear, it is not to be so!
You must stay with me, as I said before.
Your mother, too, must keep her royal state,

Since no repudiation stains this need.
Equal magnificence will orb her round
In aftertime as now. A palace here,
A palace in the country, wealth to match,
A rank in order next my future wife's,
And conference with me as my truest friend.
Now we will seek her—Eugene, you, and I—
And make the project clear.

[Exeunt NAPOLEON and HORTENSE. The scene darkens and shuts.]

SCENE III

VIENNA. A PRIVATE APARTMENT IN THE IMPERIAL PALACE

[The EMPEROR FRANCIS discovered, paler than usual, and somewhat flurried. Enter METTERNICH the
Prime Minister—a thin-lipped, long-nosed man with inquisitive eyes.]

FRANCIS
I have been expecting you some minutes here,
The thing that fronts us brooking brief delay.—
Well, what say you by now on this strange offer?

METTERNICH
My views remain the same, your Majesty:
The policy of peace that I have upheld,
Both while in Paris and of late time here,
Points to this step as heralding sweet balm
And bandaged veins for our late crimsoned realm.

FRANCIS
Agreed. As monarch I perceive therein
A happy doorway for my purposings.
It seems to guarantee the Hapsburg crown
A quittance of distractions such as those
That leave their shade on many a backward year!—
There is, forsooth, a suddenness about it,
And it would aid us had we clearly keyed
The cryptologues of which the world has heard
Between Napoleon and the Russian Court—
Begun there with the selfsame motiving.

METTERNICH
I would not, sire, one second ponder it.
It was an obvious first crude cast-about
In the important reckoning of means

For his great end, a strong monarchic line.
The more advanced the more it profits us;
For sharper, then, the quashing of such views,
And wreck of that conjunction in the aims
Of France and Russia, marked so much of late
As jeopardizing quiet neighbours' thrones.

FRANCIS
If that be so, on the domestic side
There seems no bar. Speaking as father solely,
I see secured to her the proudest fate
That woman can daydream. And I could hope
That private bliss would not be wanting her!

METTERNICH
A hope well seated, sire. The Emperor,
Imperious and determined in his rule,
Is easy-natured in domestic life,
As my long time in Paris amply proved.
Moreover, the accessories of his glory
Have been, and will be, admirably designed
To fire the fancy of a young princess.

FRANCIS
Thus far you satisfy me.... So, to close,
Or not to close with him, is now the thing.

METTERNICH
Your Majesty commands the issue quite:
The father of his people can alone
In such a case give answer—yes or no.
Vagueness and doubt have ruined Russia's chance;
Let not, then, such be ours.

FRANCIS
You mean, if I,
You'd answer straight. What would that answer be?

METTERNICH
In state affairs, sire, as in private life,
Times will arise when even the faithfullest squire
Finds him unfit to jog his chieftain's choice,
On whom responsibility must lastly rest.
And such times are pre-eminently, sire,
Those wherein thought alone is not enough
To serve the head as guide. As Emperor,
As father, both, to you, to you in sole
Must appertain the privilege to pronounce

Which track stern duty bids you tread herein.

FRANCIS
Affection is my duty, heart my guide.—
Without constraint or prompting I shall leave
The big decision in my daughter's hands.
Before my obligations to my people
Must stand her wish. Go, find her, Metternich,
Take her the tidings. She is free with you,
And will speak out. [Looking forth from the terrace.]
She's here at hand, I see:
I'll call her in. Then tell me what's her mind.

[He beckons from the window, and goes out in another direction.]

METTERNICH
So much for form's sake! Can the river-flower
The current drags, direct its face up-stream?
What she must do she will; nought else at all.

[Enter through one of the windows MARIA LOUISA in garden-costume, fresh-coloured, girlish, and smiling. METTERNICH bends.]

MARIA LOUISA
O how, dear Chancellor, you startled me!
Please pardon my so brusquely bursting in.
I saw you not.—Those five poor little birds
That haunt out there beneath the pediment,
Snugly defended from the north-east wind,
Have lately disappeared. I sought a trace
Of scattered feathers, which I dread to find!

METTERNICH
They are gone, I ween, the way of tender flesh
At the assaults of winter, want, and foes.

MARIA LOUISA
It is too melancholy thinking, that!
Don't say it.—But I saw the Emperor here?
Surely he beckoned me?

METTERNICH
Sure, he did,
Your gracious Highness; and he has left me here
To break vast news that will make good his call.

MARIA LOUISA
Then do. I'll listen. News from near or far?

[She seats herself.]

METTERNICH
From far—though of such distance-dwarfing might
That far may read as near eventually.
But, dear Archduchess, with your kindly leave
I'll speak straight out. The Emperor of the French
Has sent to-day to make, through Schwarzenberg,
A formal offer of his heart and hand,
His honours, dignities, imperial throne,
To you, whom he admires above all those
The world can show elsewhere.

MARIA LOUISA [frightened]
My husband—he?
What, an old man like him!

METTERNICH [cautiously]
He's scarcely old,
Dear lady. True, deeds densely crowd in him;
Turn months to years calendaring his span;
Yet by Time's common clockwork he's but young.

MARIA LOUISA
So wicked, too!

METTERNICH [nettled]
Well-that's a point of view.

MARIA LOUISA
But, Chancellor, think what things I have said to him!
Can women marry where they have taunted so?

METTERNICH
Things? Nothing inexpungeable, I deem,
By time and true good humour.

MARIA LOUISA
O I have!
Horrible things. Why—ay, a hundred times—
I have said I wished him dead! At that strained hour
When the first voicings of the late war came,
Thrilling out how the French were smitten sore
And Bonaparte retreating, I clapped hands
And answered that I hoped he'd lose his head
As well as lose the battle!

METTERNICH
Words. But words!
Born like the bubbles of a spring that come
Of zest for springing—aimless in their shape.

MARIA LOUISA
It seems indecent, mean, to wed a man
Whom one has held such fierce opinions of!

METTERNICH
My much beloved Archduchess, and revered,
Such things have been! In Spain and Portugal
Like enmities have led to intermarriage.
In England, after warring thirty years
The Red and White Rose wedded.

MARIA LOUISA [after a silence]
Tell me, now,
What does my father wish?

METTERNICH
His wish is yours.
Whatever your Imperial Highness feels
On this grave verdict of your destiny,
Home, title, future sphere, he bids you think
Not of himself, but of your own desire.

MARIA LOUISA [reflecting]
My wish is what my duty bids me wish.
Where a wide Empire's welfare is in poise,
That welfare must be pondered, not my will.
I ask of you, then, Chancellor Metternich,
Straightway to beg the Emperor my father
That he fulfil his duty to the realm,
And quite subordinate thereto all thought
Of how it personally impinge on me.

[A slight noise as of something falling is heard in the room. They glance momentarily, and see that a small enamel portrait of MARIE ANTOINETTE, which was standing on a console-table, has slipped down on its face.]

SPIRIT OF THE YEARS
What mischief's this? The Will must have its way.

SPIRIT SINISTER
Perhaps Earth shivered at the lady's say?

SHADE OF THE EARTH

I own hereto. When France and Austria wed
My echoes are men's groans, my dews are red;
So I have reason for a passing dread!
METTERNICH

Right nobly phrased, Archduchess; wisely too.
I will acquaint your sire the Emperor
With these your views. He waits them anxiously. [Going.]

MARIA LOUISA
Let me go first. It much confuses me
To think—But I would fain let thinking be!

[She goes out trembling. Enter FRANCIS by another door.]

METTERNICH
I was about to seek your Majesty.
The good Archduchess luminously holds
That in this weighty question you regard
The Empire. Best for it is best for her.

FRANCIS [moved]
My daughter's views thereon do not surprise me.
She is too staunch to pit a private whim
Against the fortunes of a commonwealth.
During your speech with her I have taken thought
To shape decision sagely. An assent
Would yield the Empire many years of peace,
And leave me scope to heal those still green sores
Which linger from our late unhappy moils.
Therefore, my daughter not being disinclined,
I know no basis for a negative.
Send, then, a courier prompt to Paris: say
The offer made for the Archduchess' hand
I do accept—with this defined reserve,
That no condition, treaty, bond, attach
To such alliance save the tie itself.
There are some sacrifices whose grave rites
No bargain must contaminate. This is one—
This personal gift of a beloved child!

METTERNICH [leaving]
I'll see to it this hour, your Majesty,
And cant the words in keeping with your wish.
To himself as he goes.]
Decently done!... He slipped out "sacrifice,"
And scarce could hide his heartache for his girl.
Well ached it!—But when these things have to be

It is as well to breast them stoically.

[Exit METTERNICH. The clouds draw over.]

SCENE IV

LONDON. A CLUB IN ST. JAMES'S STREET

[A winter midnight. Two members are conversing by the fire, and others are seen lolling in the background, some of them snoring.]

FIRST MEMBER
I learn from a private letter that it was carried out in the Emperor's Cabinet at the Tuileries—just off the throne-room, where they all assembled in the evening,—Boney and the wife of his bosom [In pure white muslin from head to foot, they say], the Kings and Queens of Holland, Whesthpalia, and Naples, the Princess Pauline, and one or two more; the officials present being Cambaceres the Chancellor, and Count Regnaud. Quite a small party. It was over in minutes—short and sweet, like a donkey's gallop.

SECOND MEMBER
Anything but sweet for her. How did she stand it?

FIRST MEMBER
Serenely, I believe, while the Emperor was making his speech renouncing her; but when it came to her turn to say she renounced him she began sobbing mightily, and was so completely choked up that she couldn't get out a word.

SECOND MEMBER
Poor old dame! I pity her, by God; though she had a rattling good spell while it lasted.

FIRST MEMBER
They say he was a bit upset, too, at sight of her tears But I dare vow that was put on. Fancy Boney caring a curse what a woman feels. She had learnt her speech by heart, but that did not help her: Regnaud had to finish it for her, the ditch that overturned her being where she was made to say that she no longer preserved any hope of having children, and that she was pleased to show her attachment by enabling him to obtain them by another woman. She was led off fainting. A turning of the tables, considering how madly jealous she used to make him by her flirtations!

[Enter a third member.]

SECOND MEMBER
How is the debate going? Still braying the Government in a mortar?

THIRD MEMBER
They are. Though one thing every body admits: young Peel has made a wonderful first speech in seconding the address. There has been nothing like it since Pitt. He spoke rousingly of Austria's misfortunes—went on about Spain, of course, showing that we must still go on supporting her, winding

up with a brilliant peroration about—what were the words—"the fiery eyes of the British soldier!"—Oh, well: it was all learnt before-hand, of course.

SECOND MEMBER
I wish I had gone down. But the wind soon blew the other way.

THIRD MEMBER
Then Gower rapped out his amendment. That was good, too, by God.

SECOND MEMBER
Well, the war must go on. And that being the general conviction this censure and that censure are only so many blank cartridges.

THIRD MEMBER
Blank? Damn me, were they! Gower's was a palpable hit when he said that Parliament had placed unheard-of resources in the hands of the Ministers last year, to make this year's results to the country worse than if they had been afforded no resources at all. Every single enterprise of theirs had been a beggarly failure.

SECOND MEMBER
Anybody could have said it, come to that.

THIRD MEMBER
Yes, because it is so true. However, when he began to lay on with such rhetoric as "the treasures of the nation lavished in wasteful thoughtlessness,"—"thousands of our troops sacrificed wantonly in pestilential swamps of Walcheren," and gave the details we know so well, Ministers wriggled a good one, though 'twas no news to 'em. Castlereagh kept on starting forward as if he were going to jump up and interrupt, taking the strictures entirely as a personal affront.

[Enter a fourth member.]

SEVERAL MEMBERS
Who's speaking now?

FOURTH MEMBER
I don't know. I have heard nobody later than Ward.

SECOND MEMBER
The fact is that, as Whitbread said to me to-day, the materials for condemnation are so prodigious that we can scarce marshal them into argument. We are just able to pour 'em out one upon t'other.

THIRD MEMBER
Ward said, with the blandest air in the world: "Censure? Do his Majesty's Ministers expect censure? Not a bit. They are going about asking in tremulous tones if anybody has heard when their impeachment is going to begin."

SEVERAL MEMBERS
Haw—haw—haw!

THIRD MEMBER
Then he made another point. After enumerating our frightful failures—Spain, Walcheren, and the rest—he said: "But Ministers have not failed in everything. No; in one thing they have been strikingly successful. They have been successful in their attack upon Copenhagen—because it was directed against an ally!" Mighty fine, wasn't it?

SECOND MEMBER
How did Castlereagh stomach that?

THIRD MEMBER
He replied then. Donning his air of injured innocence he proved the honesty of his intentions—no doubt truly enough. But when he came to Walcheren nothing could be done. The case was hopeless, and he knew it, and foundered. However, at the division, when he saw what a majority was going out on his side he was as frisky as a child. Canning's speech was grave, with bits of shiny ornament stuck on—like the brass nails on a coffin, Sheridan says.

[Fifth and sixth members stagger in, arm-and-arm.]

FIFTH MEMBER
The 'vision is—'jority of ninety-six againsht—Gov'ment—I mean—againsht us. Which is it—hey? [To his companion.]

SIXTH MEMBER
Damn majority of—damn ninety-six—against damn amendment!

[They sink down on a sofa.]

SECOND MEMBER

Gad, I didn't expect the figure would have been quite so high!

THIRD MEMBER
The one conviction is that the war in the Peninsula is to go on, and as we are all agreed upon that, what the hell does it matter what their majority was?

[Enter SHERIDAN. They all look inquiringly.]

SHERIDAN
Have ye heard the latest?

SECOND MEMBER
Ninety-six against us.

SHERIDAN
O no-that's ancient history. I'd forgot it.

THIRD MEMBER

A revolution, because Ministers are not impeached and hanged?

SHERIDAN
That's in contemplation, when we've got their confessions. But what I meant was from over the water—
it is a deuced sight more serious to us than a debate and division that are only like the Liturgy on a
Sunday—known beforehand to all the congregation. Why, Bonaparte is going to marry Austria
forthwith—the Emperor's daughter Maria Louisa.

THIRD MEMBER
The Lord look down! Our late respected crony of Austria! Why, in this very night's debate they have
been talking about the laudable principles we have been acting upon in affording assistance to the
Emperor Francis in his struggle against the violence and ambition of France!

SECOND MEMBER
Boney safe on that side, what may not befall!

THIRD MEMBER
We had better make it up with him, and shake hands all round.

SECOND MEMBER
Shake heads seems most natural in the case. O House of Hapsburg, how hast thou fallen!

[Enter WHITBREAD, LORD HUTCHINSON, LORD GEORGE CAVENDISH, GEORGE PONSONBY, WINDHAM,
LORD GREY, BARING, ELLIOT, and other members, some drunk. The conversation becomes animated
and noisy; several move off to the card-room, and the scene closes.]

SCENE V

THE OLD WEST HIGHWAY OUT OF VIENNA

[The spot is where the road passes under the slopes of the Wiener Wald, with its beautiful forest
scenery.]

DUMB SHOW
A procession of enormous length, composed of eighty carriages—many of them drawn by six horses and
one by eight—and escorted by detachments of cuirassiers, yeomanry, and other cavalry, is quickening
its speed along the highway from the city.

The six-horse carriages contain a multitude of Court officials, ladies of the Court, and other Austrian
nobility. The eight-horse coach contains a rosy, blue-eyed girl of eighteen, with full red lips, round
figure, and pale auburn hair. She is MARIA LOUISA, and her eyes are red from recent weeping. The
COUNTESS DE LAZANSKY, Grand Mistress of the Household, in the carriage with her, and the other
ladies of the Palace behind, have a pale, proud, yet resigned look, as if conscious that upon their sex had
been laid the burden of paying for the peace with France. They have been played out of Vienna with
French marches, and the trifling incident has helped on their sadness.

The observer's vision being still bent on the train of vehicles and cavalry, the point of sight is withdrawn high into the air, till the huge procession on the brown road looks no more than a file of ants crawling along a strip of garden-matting. The spacious terrestrial outlook now gained shows this to be the great road across Europe from Vienna to Munich, and from Munich westerly to France.

The puny concatenation of specks being exclusively watched, the surface of the earth seems to move along in an opposite direction, and in infinite variety of hill, dale, woodland, and champaign. Bridges are crossed, ascents are climbed, plains are galloped over, and towns are reached, among them Saint Polten, where night falls.

Morning shines, and the royal crawl is resumed, and continued through Linz, where the Danube is reapproached, and the girl looks pleased to see her own dear Donau still. Presently the tower of Brannau appears, where the animated dots pause for formalities, this being the frontier; and MARIA LOUISA becomes MARIE LOUISE and a Frenchwoman, in the charge of French officials.

After many breaks and halts, during which heavy rains spread their gauzes over the scene, the roofs and houses of Munich disclose themselves, suggesting the tesserae of an irregular mosaic. A long stop is made here.

The tedious advance continues. Vine-circled Stuttgart, flat Carlsruhe, the winding Rhine, storky Strassburg, pass in panorama beneath us as the procession is followed. With Nancy and Bar-le-Duc sliding along, the scenes begin to assume a French character, and soon we perceive Chalons and ancient Rheims. The last day of the journey has dawned. Our vision flits ahead of the cortege to Courcelles, a little place which must be passed through before Soissons is reached. Here the point of sight descends to earth, and the Dumb Show ends.

SCENE VI

COURCELLES

[It is now seen to be a quiet roadside village, with a humble church in its midst, opposite to which stands an inn, the highway passing between them. Rain is still falling heavily. Not a soul is visible anywhere.

Enter from the west a plain, lonely carriage, traveling in a direction to meet the file of coaches that we have watched. It stops near the inn, and two men muffled in cloaks alight by the door away from the hostel and towards the church, as if they wished to avoid observation. Their faces are those of NAPOLEON and MURAT, his brother-in-law. Crossing the road through the mud and rain they stand in the church porch, and watch the descending drifts.]

NAPOLEON [stamping an impatient tattoo]
One gets more chilly in a wet March than in a dry, however cold, the devil if he don't! What time do you make it now? That clock doesn't go.

MURAT [drily, looking at his watch]
Yes, it does; and it is right. If clocks were to go as fast as your wishes just now it would be awkward for the rest of the world.

NAPOLEON [chuckling good-humouredly]
How we have dished the Soissons folk, with their pavilions, and purple and gold hangings for bride and bridegroom to meet in, and stately ceremonial to match, and their thousands looking on! Here we are where there's nobody. Ha, ha!

MURAT
But why should they be dished, sire? The pavilions and ceremonies were by your own orders.

NAPOLEON
Well, as the time got nearer I couldn't stand the idea of dawdling about there.

MURAT
The Soissons people will be in a deuce of a taking at being made such fools of!

NAPOLEON
So let 'em. I'll make it up with them somehow.—She can't be far off now, if we have timed her rightly.

[He peers out into the rain and listens.]

MURAT
I don't quite see how you are going to manage when she does come.
Do we go before her toward Soissons when you have greeted her here, or follow in her rear? Or what do we do?

NAPOLEON
Heavens, I know no more than you! Trust to the moment and see what happens. [A silence.] Hark— here she comes! Good little girl; up to time!

[The distant squoshing in the mud of a multitude of hoofs and wheels is succeeded by the appearance of outriders and carriages, horses and horsemen, splashed with sample clays of the districts traversed. The vehicles slow down to the inn. NAPOLEON'S face fires up, and, followed by MURAT, he rushes into the rain towards the coach that is drawn by eight horses, containing the blue-eyed girl. He holds off his hat at the carriage-window.]

MARIE LOUISE [shrinking back inside]
Ah, Heaven! Two highwaymen are upon us!

THE EQUERRY D'AUDENARDE [simultaneously]
The Emperor!

[The steps of the coach are hastily lowered, NAPOLEON, dripping, jumps in and embraces her. The startled ARCHDUCHESS, with much blushing and confusion recognizes him.]

MARIE LOUISE [tremulously, as she recovers herself]
You are so much—better looking than your portraits—that I hardly knew you! I expected you at Soissons. We are not at Soissons yet?

NAPOLEON
No, my dearest spouse, but we are together! [Calling out to the equerry.] Drive through Soissons—pass the pavilion of reception without stopping, and don't halt till we reach Compiegne.

[He sits down in the coach and is shut in, MURAT laughing silently at the scene. Exeunt carriages and riders toward Soissons.]

CHORUS OF THE IRONIC SPIRITS [aerial music]
First 'twas a finished coquette,
And now it's a raw ingenue.—
Blond instead of brunette,
An old wife doffed for a new.
She'll bring him a baby,
As quickly as maybe,
And that's what he wants her to do,
Hoo-hoo!
And that's what he wants her to do!

SPIRIT OF THE YEARS
What lewdness lip those wry-formed phantoms there!

IRONIC SPIRITS
Nay, Showman Years! With holy reverent air
We hymn the nuptials of the Imperial pair.

[The scene thickens to mist and obscures the scene.]

SCENE VII

PETERSBURG. THE PALACE OF THE EMPRESS-MOTHER

[One of the private apartments is disclosed, in which the Empress-mother and Alexander are seated.]

EMPRESS-MOTHER
So one of Austrian blood his pomp selects
To be his bride and bulwark—not our own.
Thus are you coolly shelved!

ALEXANDER
Me, mother dear?
You, faith, if I may say it dutifully!
Had all been left to me, some time ere now
He would have wedded Kate.

EMPRESS-MOTHER
How so, my son?

Catharine was plighted, and it could not be.

ALEXANDER
Rather you swiftly pledged and married her,
To let Napoleon have no chance that way.
But Anne remained.

EMPRESS-MOTHER
How Anne?—so young a girl!
Sane Nature would have cried indecency
At such a troth.

ALEXANDER
Time would have tinkered that,
And he was well-disposed to wait awhile;
But the one test he had no temper for
Was the apparent slight of unresponse
Accorded his impatient overtures
By our suspensive poise of policy.

EMPRESS-MOTHER
A backward answer is our country's card—
The special style and mode of Muscovy.
We have grown great upon it, my dear son,
And may such practice rule our centuries through!
The necks of those who rate themselves our peers
Are cured of stiffness by its potency.

ALEXANDER
The principle in this case, anyhow,
Is shattered by the facts: since none can doubt
Your policy was counted an affront,
And drove my long ally to Austria's arms,
With what result to us must yet be seen!

EMPRESS-MOTHER
May Austria win much joy of the alliance!
Marrying Napoleon is a midnight leap
For any Court in Europe, credit me,
If ever such there were! What he may carve
Upon the coming years, what murderous bolt
Hurl at the rocking Constitutions round,
On what dark planet he may land himself
In his career through space, no sage can say.

ALEXANDER
Well—possibly!... And maybe all is best
That he engrafts his lineage not on us.—

But, honestly, Napoleon none the less
Has been my friend, and I regret the dream
And fleeting fancy of a closer tie!

EMPRESS-MOTHER
Ay; your regrets are sentimental ever.
That he'll be writ no son-in-law of mine
Is no regret to me! But an affront
There is, no less, in his evasion on't,
Wherein the bourgeois quality of him
Veraciously peeps out. I would be sworn
He set his minions parleying with the twain—
Yourself and Francis—simultaneously,
Else no betrothal could have speeded so!

ALEXANDER
Despite the hazard of offence to one?

EMPRESS-MOTHER
More than the hazard; the necessity.

ALEXANDER
There's no offence to me.

EMPRESS-MOTHER
There should be, then.
I am a Romanoff by marriage merely,
But I do feel a rare belittlement
And loud laconic brow-beating herein!

ALEXANDER
No, mother, no! I am the Tsar—not you,
And I am only piqued in moderateness.
Marriage with France was near my heart—I own it—
What then? It has been otherwise ordained.

[A silence.]

EMPRESS-MOTHER
Here comes dear Anne Speak not of it before her.

[Enter the GRAND-DUCHESS, a girl of sixteen.]

ANNE
Alas! the news is that poor Prussia's queen,
Spirited Queen Louisa, once so fair,
Is slowly dying, mother! Did you know?

ALEXANDER [betraying emotion]
Ah!—such I dreaded from the earlier hints.
Poor soul—her heart was slain some time ago.

ANNE
What do you mean by that, my brother dear?

EMPRESS-MOTHER
He means, my child, that he as usual spends
Much sentiment upon the foreign fair,
And hence leaves little for his folk at home.

ALEXANDER
I mean, Anne, that her country's overthrow
Let death into her heart. The Tilsit days
Taught me to know her well, and honour her.
She was a lovely woman even then!...
Strangely, the present English Prince of Wales
Was wished to husband her. Had wishes won,
They might have varied Europe's history.

ANNE
Napoleon, I have heard, admired her once;
How he must grieve that soon she'll be no more!

EMPRESS-MOTHER
Napoleon and your brother loved her both.

[Alexander shows embarrassment.]

But whatsoever grief be Alexander's,
His will be none who feels but for himself.

ANNE
O mother, how can you mistake him so!
He worships her who is to be his wife,
The fair Archduchess Marie.

EMPRESS-MOTHER
Simple child,
As yet he has never seen her, or but barely.
That is a tactic suit, with love to match!

ALEXANDER [with vainly veiled tenderness]
High-souled Louisa;—when shall I forget
Those Tilsit gatherings in the long-sunned June!
Napoleon's gallantries deceived her quite,
Who fondly felt her pleas for Magdeburg

Had won him to its cause; the while, alas!
His cynic sense but posed in cruel play!

EMPRESS-MOTHER
Bitterly mourned she her civilities
When time unlocked the truth, that she had choked
Her indignation at his former slights
And slanderous sayings for a baseless hope,
And wrought no tittle for her country's gain.
I marvel why you mourn a frustrate tie
With one whose wiles could wring a woman so!

ALEXANDER [uneasily]
I marvel also, when I think of it!

EMPRESS-MOTHER
Don't listen to us longer, dearest Anne.

[Exit Anne.]

—You will uphold my judging by and by,
That as a suitor we are quit of him,
And that blind Austria will rue the hour
Wherein she plucks for him her fairest flower!

[The scene shuts.]

SCENE VIII

PARIS. THE GRAND GALLERY OF THE LOUVRE AND THE SALON-CARRE ADJOINING

[The view is up the middle of the Gallery, which is now a spectacle of much magnificence. Backed by the large paintings on the walls are double rows on each side of brightly dressed ladies, the pick of Imperial society, to the number of four thousand, one thousand in each row; and behind these standing up are two rows on each side of men of privilege and fashion. Officers of the Imperial Guard are dotted about as marshals.

Temporary barriers form a wide passage up the midst, leading to the Salon-Carre, which is seen through the opening to be fitted up as a chapel, with a gorgeous altar, tall candles, and cross. In front of the altar is a platform with a canopy over it. On the platform are two gilt chairs and a prie-dieu.

The expectant assembly does not continuously remain in the seats, but promenades and talks, the voices at times rising to a din amid the strains of the orchestra, conducted by the EMPEROR'S Director of Music. Refreshments in profusion are handed round, and the extemporized cathedral resolves itself into a gigantic cafe of persons of distinction under the Empire.]

SPIRIT SINISTER
All day have they been waiting for their galanty-show, and now the hour of performance is on the strike.
It may be seasonable to muse on the sixteenth Louis and the bride's great-aunt, as the nearing
procession is, I see, appositely crossing the track of the tumbril which was the last coach of that
respected lady.... It is now passing over the site of the scaffold on which she lost her head.... Now it will
soon be here.

[Suddenly the heralds enter the Gallery at the end towards the Tuileries, the spectators ranging
themselves in their places. In a moment the wedding procession of the EMPEROR and EMPRESS
becomes visible. The civil marriage having already been performed, Napoleon and Marie Louise
advance together along the vacant pathway towards the Salon-Carre, followed by the long suite of
illustrious personages, and acclamations burst from all parts of the Grand Gallery.

SPIRIT OF THE PITIES
Whose are those forms that pair in pompous train
Behind the hand-in-hand half-wedded ones,
With faces speaking sense of an adventure
Which may close well, or not so?

RECORDING ANGEL [reciting]
First there walks
The Emperor's brother Louis, Holland's King;
Then Jerome of Westphalia with his spouse;
The mother-queen, and Julie Queen of Spain,
The Prince Borghese and the Princess Pauline,
Beauharnais the Vice-King of Italy,
And Murat King of Naples, with their Queens;
Baden's Grand-Duke, Arch-Chancellor Cambaceres,
Berthier, Lebrun, and, not least, Talleyrand.
Then the Grand Marshal and the Chamberlain,
The Lords-in-Waiting, the Grand Equerry,
With waiting-ladies, women of the chamber,
An others called by office, rank, or fame.

SPIRIT OF RUMOUR
New, many, to Imperial dignities;
Which, won by character and quality
In those who now enjoy them, will become
The birthright of their sons in aftertime.

SPIRIT OF THE YEARS
It fits thee not to augur, quick-eared Shade.
Ephemeral at the best all honours be,
These even more ephemeral than their kind,
So random-fashioned, swift, perturbable!

SPIRIT OF THE PITIES
Napoleon looks content—nay, shines with joy.

SPIRIT OF THE YEARS
Yet see it pass, as by a conjuror's wand.

[Thereupon Napoleon's face blackens as if the shadow of a winter night had fallen upon it. Resentful and threatening, he stops the procession and looks up and down the benches.]

SPIRIT SINISTER
This is sound artistry of the Immanent Will: it relieves the monotony of so much good-humour.

NAPOLEON [to the Chapel-master]
Where are the Cardinals? And why not here? [He speaks so loud that he is heard throughout the Gallery.]

ABBE DE PRADT [trembling]
Many are present here, your Majesty;
But some are feebled by infirmities
Too common to their age, and cannot come.

NAPOLEON
Tell me no nonsense! Half absent themselves
Because they WILL not come. The factious fools!
Well, be it so. But they shall flinch for it!

[MARIE LOUISE looks frightened. The procession moves on.]

SPIRIT OF THE PITIES
I seem to see the thin and headless ghost
Of the yet earlier Austrian, here, too, queen,
Walking beside the bride, with frail attempts
To pluck her by the arm!

SPIRIT OF THE YEARS
Nay, think not so.
No trump unseals earth's sepulchre's to-day:
We are the only phantoms now abroad
On this mud-moulded ball! Through sixteen years
She has decayed in a back-garden yonder,
Dust all the showance time retains of her,
Senseless of hustlings in her former house,
Lost to all count of crowns and bridalry—
Even of her Austrian blood. No: what thou seest
Springs of the quavering fancy, stirred to dreams
By yon tart phantom's phrase.

MARIE LOUISE [sadly to Napoleon]
I know not why,
I love not this day's doings half so well

As our quaint meeting-time at Compiegne.
A clammy air creeps round me, as from vaults
Peopled with looming spectres, chilling me
And angering you withal!

NAPOLEON
O, it is nought
To trouble you: merely, my cherished one,
Those devils of Italian Cardinals!—
Now I'll be bright as ever—you must, too.

MARIE LOUISE
I'll try.

[Reaching the entrance to the Salon-Carre amid strains of music the EMPEROR and EMPRESS are
received and incensed by the CARDINAL GRAND ALMONERS. They take their seats under the canopy,
and the train of notabilities seat themselves further back, the persons-in-waiting stopping behind the
Imperial chairs.

The ceremony of the religious marriage now begins. The choir intones a hymn, the EMPEROR and
EMPRESS go to the altar, remove their gloves, and make their vows.]

SPIRIT IRONIC
The English Church should return thanks for this wedding, seeing how it will purge of coarseness the
picture-sheets of that artistic nation, which will hardly be able to caricature the new wife as it did poor
plebeian Josephine. Such starched and ironed monarchists cannot sneer at a woman of such a divinely
dry and crusted line like the Hapsburgs!

[Mass is next celebrated, after which the TE DEUM is chanted in harmonies that whirl round the walls of
the Salon-Carre and quiver down the long Gallery. The procession then re-forms and returns, amid the
flutterings and applause of the dense assembly. But Napoleon's face has not lost the sombre expression
which settled on it. The pair and their train pass out by the west door, and the congregation disperses in
the other direction, the cloud-curtain closing over the scene as they disappear.

ACT SIXTH

SCENE I

THE LINES OF TORRES VEDRAS

[A bird's-eye perspective is revealed of the peninsular tract of Portuguese territory lying between the
shining pool of the Tagus on the east, and the white-frilled Atlantic lifting rhythmically on the west. As
thus beheld the tract features itself somewhat like a late-Gothic shield, the upper edge from the dexter
to the sinister chief being the lines of Torres Vedras, stretching across from the mouth of the Zezambre
on the left to Alhandra on the right, and the south or base point being Fort S. Julian. The roofs of Lisbon

appear at the sinister base, and in a corresponding spot on the opposite side Cape Roca.

It is perceived in a moment that the northern verge of this nearly coast-hemmed region is the only one through which access can be gained to it by land, and a close scrutiny of the boundary there reveals that means are being adopted to effectually prevent such access.

From east to west along it runs a chain of defences, dotted at intervals by dozens of circular and square redoubts, either made or in the making, two of the latter being of enormous size. Between these stretch unclimbable escarpments, stone walls, and other breastworks, and in front of all a double row of abatis, formed of the limbs of trees.

Within the outer line of defence is a second, constructed on the same shield-shaped tract of country; and is not more than a twelfth of the length of the others. It is a continuous entrenchment of ditches and ramparts, and its object—that of covering a forced embarkation—is rendered apparent by some rocking English transports off the shore hard by.]

DUMB SHOW
Innumerable human figures are busying themselves like cheese-mites all along the northernmost frontage, undercutting easy slopes into steep ones, digging ditches, piling stones, felling trees, dragging them, and interlacing them along the front as required.

On the second breastwork, which is completed, only a few figures move.

On the third breastwork, which is fully matured and equipped, minute red sentinels creep backwards and forwards noiselessly.

As time passes three reddish-grey streams of marching men loom out to the north, advancing southward along three roads towards three diverse points in the first defence. These form the English army, entering the lines for shelter. Looked down upon, their motion seems peristaltic and vermicular, like that of three caterpillars.

The division on the left is under Picton, in the centre under Leith and Cole, and on the extreme right, by Alhandra, under Hill. Beside one of the roads two or three of the soldiers are dangling from a tree by the neck, probably for plundering.

The Dumb Show ends, and the point of view sinks to the earth.

SCENE II

THE SAME. OUTSIDE THE LINES

[The winter day has gloomed to a stormful evening, and the road outside the first line of defence forms the foreground of the stage.

Enter in the dusk from the hills to the north of the entrenchment, near Calandrix, a group of horsemen, which includes MASSENA in command of the French forces, FOY, LOISON, and other officers of his staff.

They ride forward in the twilight and tempest, and reconnoitre, till they see against the sky the ramparts blocking the road they pursue. They halt silently. MASSENA, puzzled, endeavours with his glass to make out the obstacle.]

MASSENA
Something stands here to peril our advance,
Or even prevent it!

FOY
These are the English lines—
Their outer horns and tusks—whereof I spoke,
Constructed by Lord Wellington of late
To keep his foothold firm in Portugal.

MASSENA
Thrusts he his burly, bossed disfigurements
So far to north as this? I had pictured me
The lay much nearer Lisbon. Little strange
Lord Wellington rode placid at Busaco
With this behind his back! Well, it is hard
But that we turn them somewhere, I assume?
They scarce can close up every southward gap
Between the Tagus and the Atlantic Sea.

FOY
I hold they can, and do; although, no doubt,
By searching we shall spy some raggedness
Which customed skill may force.

MASSENA
Plain 'tis, no less,
We may heap corpses vainly hereabout,
And crack good bones in waste. By human power
This passes mounting! What say you's behind?

LOISON
Another line exactly like the first,
But more matured. Behind its back a third.

MASSENA
How long have these prim ponderosities
Been rearing up their foreheads to the moon?

LOISON
Some months in all. I know not quite how long.
They are Lord Wellington's select device,
And, like him, heavy, slow, laborious, sure.

MASSENA
May he enjoy their sureness. He deserves to.
I had no inkling of such barriers here.
A good road runs along their front, it seems,
Which offers us advantage.... What a night!

[The tempest cries dismally about the earthworks above them, as the reconnoitrers linger in the slight shelter the lower ground affords. They are about to turn back.

Enter from the cross-road to the right JUNOT and some more officers. They come up at a signal that the others are those they lately parted from.]

JUNOT
We have ridden along as far as Calandrix,
Favoured therein by this disordered night,
Which tongues its language to the disguise of ours;
And find amid the vale an open route
That, well manoeuvred, may be practicable.

MASSENA
I'll look now at it, while the weather aids.
If it may serve our end when all's prepared
So good. If not, some other to the west.

[Exeunt MASSENA, JUNOT, LOISON, FOY, and the rest by the paved crossway to the right.

The wind continues to prevail as the spot is left desolate, the darkness increases, rain descends more heavily, and the scene is blotted out.]

SCENE III

PARIS. THE TUILERIES

[The anteroom to the EMPRESS MARIE LOUISE'S bed-chamber, in which are discovered NAPOLEON in his dressing-gown, the DUCHESS OF MONTEBELLO, and other ladies-in-waiting. CORVISART the first physician, and the second physician BOURDIER.

The time is before dawn. The EMPEROR walks up and down, throws himself on a sofa, or stands at the window. A cry of anguish comes occasionally from within.

NAPOLEON opens the door and speaks into the bed-chamber.]

NAPOLEON
How now, Dubois?

VOICE OF DUBOIS THE ACCOUCHEUR [nervously]
Less well, sire, than I hoped;
I fear no skill can save them both.

NAPOLEON [agitated]
Good god!

[Exit CORVISART into the bed-room. Enter DUBOIS.]

DUBOIS [with hesitation]
Which life is to be saved? The Empress, sire,
Lies in great jeopardy. I have not known
In my long years of many-featured practice
An instance in a thousand fall out so.

NAPOLEON
Then save the mother, pray! Think but of her;
It is her privilege, and my command.—
Don't lose you head, Dubois, at this tight time:
Your furthest skill can work but what it may.
Fancy that you are merely standing by
A shop-wife's couch, say, in the Rue Saint Denis;
Show the aplomb and phlegm that you would show
Did such a bed receive your ministry.

[Exit DUBOIS.]

VOICE OF MARIE LOUISE [within]
O pray, pray don't! Those ugly things terrify me! Why should I be tortured even if I am but a means to
an end! Let me die! It was cruel of him to bring this upon me!

[Exit NAPOLEON impatiently to the bed-room.]

VOICE OF MADAME DE MONTESQUIOU [within]
Keep up your spirits, madame! I have been through it myself and I assure you there is no danger to you.
It is going on all right, and I am holding you.

VOICE OF NAPOLEON [within]
Heaven above! Why did you not deep those cursed sugar-tongs out of her sight? How is she going to
get through it if you frighten her like this?

VOICE OF DUBOIS [within]
If you will pardon me, your Majesty,
I must implore you not to interfere!
I'll not be scapegoat for the consequence
If, sire, you do! Better for her sake far
Would you withdraw. The sight of your concern
But agitates and weakens her endurance.

I will inform you all, and call you back
If things should worsen here.

[Re-enter NAPOLEON from the bed-chamber. He half shuts the door, and remains close to it listening, pale and nervous.]

BOURDIER
I ask you, sire,
To harass yourself less with this event,
Which may amend anon: I much regret
The honoured mother of your Majesty,
And sister too, should both have left ere now,
Whose solace would have bridged these anxious hours.

NAPOLEON [absently]
As we were not expecting it so soon
I begged they would sit up no longer here....
She ought to get along; she has help enough
With that half-dozen of them at hand within—
Skilled Madame Blaise the nurse, and two besides,
Madame de Montesquiou and Madame Ballant—

DUBOIS [speaking through the doorway]
Past is the question, sire, of which to save!
The child is dead; the while her Majesty
Is getting through it well.

NAPOLEON
Praise Heaven for that!
I'll not grieve overmuch about the child....
Never shall She go through this strain again
To lay down a dynastic line for me.

DUCHESS OF MONTEBELLO [aside to the second lady]
He only says that now. In cold blood it would be far otherwise.
That's how men are.

VOICE OF MADAME BLAISE [within]
Doctor, the child's alive! [The cry of an infant is heard.]

VOICE OF DUBOIS [calling from within]
Sire, both are saved.

[NAPOLEON rushes into the chamber, and is heard kissing MARIE LOUISE.]

VOICE OF MADAME BLAISE [within]
A vigorous boy, your Imperial Majesty. The brandy and hot napkins brought him to.

DUCHESS OF MONTEBELLO
It is as I expected. A healthy young woman of her build had every chance of doing well, despite the doctors.

[An interval.]

NAPOLEON [re-entering radiantly]
We have achieved a healthy heir, good dames,
And in the feat the Empress was most brave,
Although she suffered much—so much, indeed,
That I would sooner father no more sons
Than have so fair a fruit-tree undergo
Another wrenching of such magnitude.

[He walks to the window, pulls aside the curtains, and looks out. It is a joyful spring morning. The Tuileries' gardens are thronged with an immense crowd, kept at a little distance off the Palace by a cord. The windows of the neighbouring houses are full of gazers, and the streets are thronged with halting carriages, their inmates awaiting the event.]

SPIRIT OF THE YEARS [whispering to Napoleon]
At this high hour there broods a woman nigh,
Ay, here in Paris, with her child and thine,
Who might have played this part with truer eye
To thee and to thy contemplated line!

NAPOLEON [soliloquizing]
Strange that just now there flashes on my soul
That little one I loved in Warsaw days,
Marie Walewska, and my boy by her!—
She was shown faithless by a foul intrigue
Till fate sealed up her opportunity....
But what's one woman's fortune more or less
Beside the schemes of kings!—Ah, there's the new!

[A gun is heard from the Invalides.]

CROWD [excitedly]
One!

[Another report of the gun, and another, succeed.]

Two! Three! Four!

[The firing and counting proceed to twenty-one, when there is great suspense. The gun fires again, and the excitement is doubled.]

Twenty-two! A boy!

[The remainder of the counting up to a hundred-and-one is drowned in the huzzas. Bells begin ringing, and from the Champ de Mars a balloon ascends, from which the tidings are scattered in hand-bills as it floats away from France.

Enter the PRESIDENT OF THE SENATE, CAMBACERES, BERTHIER, LEBRUN, and other officers of state. NAPOLEON turns from the window.]

CAMBACERES
Unstinted gratulations and goodwill
We bring to your Imperial Majesty,
While still resounds the superflux of joy
With which your people welcome this live star
Upon the horizon of history!

PRESIDENT OF THE SENATE
All blessings at their goodliest will grace
The advent of this New Messiah, sire,
Of fairer prospects than the former one,
Whose coming at so apt an hour endues
The widening glory of your high exploits
With permanence, and flings the dimness far
That cloaked the future of our chronicle!

NAPOLEON
My thanks; though, gentlemen, upon my soul
You might have drawn the line at the Messiah.
But I excuse you.—Yes, the boy has come;
He took some coaxing, but he's here at last.—
And what news brings the morning from without?
I know of none but this the Empress now
Trumps to the world from the adjoining room.

PRESIDENT OF THE SENATE
Nothing in Europe, sire, that can compare
In magnitude therewith to more effect
Than with an eagle some frail finch or wren.
To wit: the ban on English trade prevailing,
Subjects our merchant-houses to such strain
That many of the best see bankruptcy
Like a grim ghost ahead. Next week, they say
In secret here, six of the largest close.

NAPOLEON
It shall not be! Our burst of natal joy
Must not be sullied by so mean a thing:
Aid shall be rendered. Much as we may suffer,
England must suffer more, and I am content.
What has come in from Spain and Portugal?

BERTHIER
Vaguely-voiced rumours, sire, but nothing more,
Which travel countries quick as earthquake thrills,
No mortal knowing how.

NAPOLEON
Of Massena?

BERTHIER
Yea. He retreats for prudence' sake, it seems,
Before Lord Wellington. Dispatches soon
Must reach your Majesty, explaining all.

NAPOLEON
Ever retreating! Why declines he so
From all his olden prowess? Why, again,
Did he give battle at Busaco lately,
When Lisbon could be marched on without strain?
Why has he dallied by the Tagus bank
And shunned the obvious course? I gave him Ney,
Soult, and Junot, and eighty thousand men,
And he does nothing. Really it might seem
As though we meant to let this Wellington
Be even with us there!

BERTHIER
His mighty forts
At Torres Vedras hamper Massena,
And quite preclude advance.

NAPOLEON
O well—no matter:
Why should I linger on these haps of war
Now that I have a son!

[Exeunt NAPOLEON by one door and by another the PRESIDENT OF THE SENATE, CAMBACERES, LEBRUN, BERTHIER, and officials.]

CHORUS OF IRONIC SPIRITS [aerial music]
The Will Itself is slave to him,
And holds it blissful to obey!—
He said, "Go to; it is my whim

"To bed a bride without delay,
Who shall unite my dull new name
With one that shone in Caesar's day.

"She must conceive—you hear my claim?—
And bear a son—no daughter, mind—
Who shall hand on my form and fame

"To future times as I have designed;
And at the birth throughout the land
Must cannon roar and alp-horns wind!"

The Will grew conscious at command,
And ordered issue as he planned.

[The interior of the Palace is veiled.]

SCENE IV

SPAIN. ALBUERA

[The dawn of a mid-May day in the same spring shows the village of Albuera with the country around it, as viewed from the summit of a line of hills on which the English and their allies are ranged under Beresford. The landscape swept by the eye includes to the right foreground a hill loftier than any, and somewhat detached from the range. The green slopes behind and around this hill are untrodden—though in a few hours to be the sanguinary scene of the most murderous struggle of the whole war.

The village itself lies to the left foreground, with its stream flowing behind it in the distance on the right. A creeping brook at the bottom of the heights held by the English joins the stream by the village. Behind the stream some of the French forces are visible. Away behind these stretches a great wood several miles in area, out of which the Albuera stream emerges, and behind the furthest verge of the wood the morning sky lightens momently. The birds in the wood, unaware that this day is to be different from every other day they have known there, are heard singing their overtures with their usual serenity.]

DUMB SHOW
As objects grow more distinct it can be perceived that some strategic dispositions of the night are being completed by the French forces, which the evening before lay in the woodland to the front of the English army. They have emerged during the darkness, and large sections of them—infantry, cuirassiers, and artillery—have crept round to BERESFORD'S right without his suspecting the movement, where they lie hidden by the great hill aforesaid, though not more than half-a-mile from his right wing.

SPIRIT OF THE YEARS
A hot ado goes forward here to-day,
If I may read the Immanent Intent
From signs and tokens blent
With weird unrest along the firmament
Of causal coils in passionate display.
—Look narrowly, and what you witness say.

SPIRIT OF THE PITIES

I see red smears upon the sickly dawn,
And seeming drops of gore. On earth below
Are men—unnatural and mechanic-drawn—
Mixt nationalities in row and row,
Wheeling them to and fro
In moves dissociate from their souls' demand,
For dynasts' ends that few even understand!

SPIRIT OF THE YEARS
Speak more materially, and less in dream.

SPIRIT OF RUMOUR
I'll do it.... The stir of strife grows well defined
Around the hamlet and the church thereby:
Till, from the wood, the ponderous columns wind,
Guided by Godinot, with Werle nigh.
They bear upon the vill. But the gruff guns
Of Dickson's Portuguese
Punch spectral vistas through the maze of these!...
More Frenchmen press, and roaring antiphons
Of cannonry contuse the roofs and walls and trees.

SPIRIT OF THE PITIES
Wrecked are the ancient bridge, the green spring plot,
the blooming fruit-tree, the fair flower-knot!

SPIRIT OF RUMOUR
Yet the true mischief to the English might
Is meant to fall not there. Look to the right,
And read the shaping scheme by yon hill-side,
Where cannon, foot, and brisk dragoons you see,
With Werle and Latour-Maubourg to guide,
Waiting to breast the hill-brow bloodily.

BERESFORD now becomes aware of this project on his flank, and sends orders to throw back his right to
face the attack. The order is not obeyed. Almost at the same moment the French rush is made, the
Spanish and Portuguese allies of the English are beaten beck, and the hill is won. But two English
divisions bear from the centre of their front, and plod desperately up the hill to retake it.

SPIRIT SINISTER
Now he among us who may wish to be
A skilled practitioner in slaughtery,
Should watch this hour's fruition yonder there,
And he will know, if knowing ever were,
How mortals may be freed their fleshly cells,
And quaint red doors set ope in sweating fells,
By methods swift and slow and foul and fair!

The English, who have plunged up the hill, are caught in a heavy mist, that hides from them an advance in their rear of the lancers and hussars of the enemy. The lines of the Buffs, the Sixty-sixth, and those of the Forty-eighth, who were with them, in a chaos of smoke, steel, sweat, curses, and blood, are beheld melting down like wax from an erect position to confused heaps. Their forms lie rigid, or twitch and turn, as they are trampled over by the hoofs of the enemy's horse. Those that have not fallen are taken.

SPIRIT OF THE PITIES
It works as you, uncanny Phantom, wist!...
Whose is that towering form
That tears across the mist
To where the shocks are sorest?—his with arm
Outstretched, and grimy face, and bloodshot eye,
Like one who, having done his deeds, will die?

SPIRIT OF RUMOUR
He is one Beresford, who heads the fight
For England here to-day.

SPIRIT OF THE PITIES
He calls the sight
Despite itself!—parries yon lancer's thrust,
And with his own sword renders dust to dust!

The ghastly climax of the strife is reached; the combatants are seen to be firing grape and canister at speaking distance, and discharging musketry in each other's faces when so close that their complexions may be recognized. Hot corpses, their mouths blackened by cartridge-biting, and surrounded by cast-away knapsacks, firelocks, hats, stocks, flint-boxes, and priming horns, together with red and blue rags of clothing, gaiters, epaulettes, limbs and viscera accumulate on the slopes, increasing from twos and threes to half-dozens, and from half-dozens to heaps, which steam with their own warmth as the spring rain falls gently upon them.

The critical instant has come, and the English break. But a comparatively fresh division, with fusileers, is brought into the turmoil by HARDINGE and COLE, and these make one last strain to save the day, and their names and lives. The fusileers mount the incline, and issuing from the smoke and mist startle the enemy by their arrival on a spot deemed won.

SEMICHORUS I OF THE PITIES [aerial music]
They come, beset by riddling hail;
They sway like sedges is a gale;
The fail, and win, and win, and fail. Albuera!

SEMICHORUS II
They gain the ground there, yard by yard,
Their brows and hair and lashes charred,
Their blackened teeth set firm and hard.

SEMICHORUS I
Their mad assailants rave and reel,

And face, as men who scorn to feel,
The close-lined, three-edged prongs of steel.

SEMICHORUS II
Till faintness follows closing-in,
When, faltering headlong down, they spin
Like leaves. But those pay well who win Albuera.

SEMICHORUS I
Out of six thousand souls that sware
To hold the mount, or pass elsewhere,
But eighteen hundred muster there.

SEMICHORUS II
Pale Colonels, Captains, ranksmen lie,
Facing the earth or facing sky;—
They strove to live, they stretch to die.

SEMICHORUS I
Friends, foemen, mingle; heap and heap.—
Hide their hacked bones, Earth!—deep, deep, deep,
Where harmless worms caress and creep.

CHORUS
Hide their hacked bones, Earth!—deep, deep, deep,
Where harmless worms caress and creep.—
What man can grieve? what woman weep?
Better than waking is to sleep! Albuera!
The night comes on, and darkness covers the battle-field.

SCENE V

WINDSOR CASTLE. A ROOM IN THE KING'S APARTMENT

[The walls of the room are padded, and also the articles of furniture, the stuffing being overlaid with satin and velvet, on which are worked in gold thread monograms and crowns. The windows are guarded, and the floor covered with thick cork, carpeted. The time is shortly after the last scene.

The KING is seated by a window, and two of Dr. WILLIS'S attendants are in the room. His MAJESTY is now seventy-two; his sight is very defective, but he does not look ill. He appears to be lost in melancholy thought, and talks to himself reproachfully, hurried manner on occasion being the only irregular symptom that he betrays.]

KING

In my lifetime I did not look after her enough—enough—enough! And now she is lost to me, and I shall never see her more. Had I but known, had I but thought of it! Gentlemen, when did I lose the Princess Amelia?

FIRST ATTENDANT
The second of last November, your Majesty.

KING
And what is it now?

FIRST ATTENDANT
Now, sir, it is the beginning of June.

KING
Ah, June, I remember!... The June flowers are not for me. I shall never see them; nor will she. So fond of them as she was.... Even if I were living I would never go where there are flowers any more! No: I would go to the bleak, barren places that she never would walk in, and never knew, so that nothing might remind me of her, and make my heart ache more than I can bear!... Why, the beginning of June?—that's when they are coming to examine me!

[He grows excited.]

FIRST ATTENDANT [to second attendant, aside]
Dr. Reynolds ought not have reminded him of their visit. It only disquiets him and makes him less fit to see them.

KING
How long have I been confined here?

FIRST ATTENDANT
Since November, sir; for your health's sake entirely, as your Majesty knows.

KING
What, what? So long? Ah, yes. I must bear it. This is the fourth great black gulf in my poor life, is it not? The fourth.

[A signal from the door. The second attendant opens it and whispers. Enter softly SIR HENRY HALFORD, DR. WILLIAM HEBERDEN, DR. ROBERT WILLIS, DR. MATTHEW BAILLIE, the KING'S APOTHECARY, and one or two other gentlemen.]

KING [straining his eye to discern them]
What! Are they come? What will they do to me? How dare they! I am Elector of Hanover! [Finding Dr. Willis is among them he shrieks.] O, they are going to bleed me—yes, to bleed me! [Piteously.] My friends, don't bleed me—pray don't! It makes me so weak to take my blood. And the leeches do, too, when you put so many. You will not be so unkind, I am sure!

WILLIS [to Baillie]

It is extraordinary what a vast aversion he has to bleeding—that most salutary remedy, fearlessly practised. He submits to leeches as yet but I won't say that he will for long without being strait-jacketed.

KING [catching some of the words]
You will strait-jacket me? O no, no!

WILLIS
Leeches are not effective, really. Dr. Home, when I mentioned it to him yesterday, said he would bleed him till he fainted if he had charge of him!

KING
O will you do it, sir, against my will,
And put me, once your king, in needless pain?
I do assure you truly, my good friends,
That I have done no harm! In sunnier years
Ere I was throneless, withered to a shade,
Deprived of my divine authority—
When I was hale, and ruled the English land—
I ever did my utmost to promote
The welfare of my people, body and soul!
Right many a morn and night I have prayed and mused
How I could bring them to a better way.
So much of me you surely know, my friends,
And will not hurt me in my weakness here! [He trembles.]

SPIRIT OF THE PITIES
The tears that lie about this plightful scene
Of heavy travail in a suffering soul,
Mocked with the forms and teints of royalty
While scarified by briery Circumstance,
Might drive Compassion past her patiency
To hold that some mean, monstrous ironist
Had built this mistimed fabric of the Spheres
To watch the throbbings of its captive lives,
[The which may Truth forfend], and not thy said
Unmaliced, unimpassioned, nescient Will!

SPIRIT OF THE YEARS
Mild one, be not touched with human fate.
Such is the Drama: such the Mortal state:
No sigh of thine can null the Plan Predestinate!

HALFORD
We have come to do your Majesty no harm.
Here's Dr. Heberden, whom I am sure you like,
And this is Dr. Baillie. We arrive
But to inquire and gather how you are,

Thereon to let the Privy Council know,
And give assurances for you people's good.

[A brass band is heard playing in the distant part of Windsor.]

KING
Ah—what does that band play for here to-day?
She has been dead and I so short a time!...
Her little hands are hardly cold as yet;
But they can show such cruel indecency
As to let trumpets play!

HALFORD
They guess not, sir,
That you can hear them, or their chords would cease.
Their boisterous music fetches back to me
That, of our errands to your Majesty,
One was congratulation most sincere
Upon this glorious victory you have won.
The news is just in port; the band booms out
To celebrate it, and to honour you.

KING
A victory? I? Pray where?

HALFORD
Indeed so, sir:
Hard by Albuera—far in harried Spain—
Yes, sir; you have achieved a victory
Of dash unmatched and feats unparalleled!

KING
He says I have won a battle? But I thought
I was a poor afflicted captive here,
In darkness lingering out my lonely days,
Beset with terror of these myrmidons
That suck my blood like vampires! Ay, ay, ay!—
No aims left to me but to quicken death
To quicklier please my son!—And yet he says
That I have won a battle! O God, curse, damn!
When will the speech of the world accord with truth,
And men's tongues roll sincerely!

GENTLEMAN [aside]
Faith, 'twould seem
As if the madman were the sanest here!

[The KING'S face has flushed, and he becomes violent. The attendants rush forward to him.]

SPIRIT OF THE PITIES
Something within me aches to pray
To some Great Heart, to take away
This evil day, this evil day!

CHORUS IRONIC
Ha-ha! That's good. Thou'lt pray to It:—
But where do Its compassions sit?
Yea, where abides the heart of it?

Is it where sky-fires flame and flit,
Or solar craters spew and spit,
Or ultra-stellar night-webs knit?

What is Its shape? Man's counterfeit?
That turns in some far sphere unlit
The Wheel which drives the Infinite?

SPIRIT OF THE PITIES
Mock on, mock on! Yet I'll go pray
To some Great Heart, who haply may
Charm mortal miseries away!

[The KING'S paroxysm continues. The attendants hold him.]

HALFORD
This is distressing. One can never tell
How he will take things now. I thought Albuera
A subject that would surely solace him.
These paroxysms—have they been bad this week? [To Attendants.]

FIRST ATTENDANT
Sir Henry, no. He has quite often named
The late Princess, as gently as a child
A little bird found starved.

WILLIS [aside to apothecary]
I must increase the opium to-night, and lower him by a double set of leeches since he won't stand the lancet quietly.

APOTHECARY
You should take twenty ounces, doctor, if a drop—indeed, go on blooding till he's unconscious. He is too robust by half. And the watering-pot would do good again—not less than six feet above his head. See how heated he is.

WILLIS
Curse that town band. It will have to be stopped.

HEBERDEN
The same thing is going on all over England, no doubt, on account of this victory.

HALFORD
When he is in a more domineering mood he likes such allusions to his rank as king.... If he could resume his walks on the terrace he might improve slightly. But it is too soon yet. We must consider what we shall report to the Council. There is little hope of his being much better. What do you think, Willis?

WILLIS
None. He is done for this time!

HALFORD
Well, we must soften it down a little, so as not to upset the Queen too much, poor woman, and distract the Council unnecessarily. Eldon will go pumping up bucketfuls, and the Archbishops are so easily shocked that a certain conventional reserve is almost forced upon us.

WILLIS [returning from the King]
He is already better. The paroxysm has nearly passed. Your opinion will be far more favourable before you leave.

[The KING soon grows calm, and the expression of his face changes to one of dejection. The attendants leave his side: he bends his head, and covers his face with his hand, while his lips move as if in prayer. He then turns to them.]

KING [meekly]
I am most truly sorry, gentlemen,
If I have used language that would seem to show
Discourtesy to you for your good help
In this unhappy malady of mine!
My nerves unstring, my friend; my flesh grows weak:
"The good that I do I leave undone,
The evil which I would not, that I do!"
Shame, shame on me!

WILLIS [aside to the others]
Now he will be as low as before he was in the other extreme.

KING
A king should bear him kingly; I of all,
One of so long a line. O shame on me!...
—This battle that you speak of?—Spain, of course?
Ah—Albuera! And many fall—eh? Yes?

HALFORD
Many hot hearts, sir, cold, I grieve to say.
There's Major-General Houghton, Captain Bourke,
And Herbert of the Third, Lieutenant Fox,

And Captains Erck and Montague, and more.
With Majors-General Cole and Stewart wounded,
And Quartermaster-General Wallace too:
A total of three generals, colonels five,
Five majors, fifty captains; and to these
Add ensigns and lieutenants sixscore odd,
Who went out, but returned not. Heavily tithed
Were the attenuate battalions there
Who stood and bearded Death by the hour that day!

KING
O fearful price for victory! Add thereto
All those I lost at Walchere.—A crime
Lay there!... I stood on Chatham's being sent:
It wears on me, till I am unfit to live!

WILLIS [aside to the others]
Don't let him get on that Walcheren business. There will be another outbreak. Heberden, please ye talk
to him. He fancies you most.

HEBERDEN
I'll tell him some of the brilliant feats of the battle.

[He goes and talks to the KING.]

WILLIS [to the rest]

Well, my inside begins to cry cupboard. I had breakfast early. We have enough particulars now to face
the Queen's Council with, I should say, Sir Henry?

HALFORD
Yes.—I want to get back to town as soon as possible to-day. Mrs Siddons has a party at her house at
Westbourne to-night, and all the world is going to be there.

BAILLIE
Well, I am not. But I have promised to take some friends to Vauxhall, as it is a grand gala and fireworks
night. Miss Farren is going to sing "The Canary Bird."—The Regent's fete, by the way, is postponed till
the nineteenth, on account of this relapse. Pretty grumpy he was at having to do it. All the world will be
THERE, sure!

WILLIS
And some from the Shades, too, of the fair, sex.—Well, here comes
Heberden. He has pacified his Majesty nicely. Now we can get away.

[The physicians withdraw softly, and the scene is covered.]

SCENE VI

LONDON. CARLTON HOUSE AND THE STREETS ADJOINING

[It is a cloudless midsummer evening, and as the west fades the stars beam down upon the city, the evening-star hanging like a jonquil blossom. They are dimmed by the unwonted radiance which spreads around and above Carlton House. As viewed from aloft the glare rises through the skylights, floods the forecourt towards Pall Mall, and kindles with a diaphanous glow the huge tents in the gardens that overlook the Mall. The hour has arrived of the Prince Regent's festivity.

A stream of carriages and sedan-chairs, moving slowly, stretches from the building along Pall Mall into Piccadilly and Bond Street, and crowds fill the pavements watching the bejewelled and feathered occupants. In addition to the grand entrance inside the Pall Mall colonnade there is a covert little "chair-door" in Warwick Street for sedans only, by which arrivals are perceived to be slipping in almost unobserved.]

SPIRIT IRONIC
What domiciles are those, of singular expression,
Whence no guest comes to join the gemmed procession;
That, west of Hyde, this, in the Park-side Lane,
Each front beclouded like a mask of pain?

SPIRIT OF RUMOUR
Therein the princely host's two spouses dwell;
A wife in each. Let me inspect and tell.

[The walls of the two houses—one in Park Lane, the other at Kensington—become transparent.]

I see within the first his latter wife—
That Caroline of Brunswick whose brave sire
Yielded his breath on Jena's reeking plain,
And of whose kindred other yet may fall
Ere long, if character indeed be fate.—
She idles feasting, and is full of jest
As each gay chariot rumbles to the rout.
"I rank like your Archbishops' wives," laughs she;
"Denied my husband's honours. Funny me!"

[Suddenly a Beau on his way to the Carlton House festival halts at her house, calls, and is shown in.]

He brings her news that a fresh favourite rules
Her husband's ready heart; likewise of those
Obscure and unmissed courtiers late deceased,
Who have in name been bidden to the feast
By blundering scribes.

[The Princess is seen to jump up from table at some words from her visitor, and clap her hands.]

These tidings, juxtaposed,
Have fired her hot with curiosity,
And lit her quick invention with a plan.

PRINCESS OF WALES
Mine God, I'll go disguised—in some dead name
And enter by the leetle, sly, chair-door
Designed for those not welcomed openly.
There unobserved I'll note mine new supplanter!
'Tis indiscreet? Let indiscretion rule,
Since caution pensions me so scurvily!

SPIRIT IRONIC
Good. Now for the other sweet and slighted spouse.

SPIRIT OF RUMOUR
The second roof shades the Fitzherbert Fair;
Reserved, perverse. As coach and coach roll by
She mopes within her lattice; lampless, lone,
As if she grieved at her ungracious fate,
And yet were loth to kill the sting of it
By frankly forfeiting the Prince and town.
"Bidden," says she, "but as one low of rank,
And go I will not so unworthily,
To sit with common dames!"—A flippant friend
Writes then that a new planet sways to-night
The sense of her erratic lord; whereon
The fair Fitzherbert muses hankeringly.

MRS. FITZHERBERT [soliloquizing]
The guest-card which I publicly refused
Might, as a fancy, privately be used!...
Yes—one last look—a wordless, wan farewell
To this false life which glooms me like a knell,
And him, the cause; from some hid nook survey
His new magnificence;—then go for aye!

SPIRIT OF RUMOUR
She cloaks and veils, and in her private chair
Passes the Princess also stealing there—
Two honest wives, and yet a differing pair!

SPIRIT IRONIC
With dames of strange repute, who bear a ticket
For screened admission by the private wicket.

CHORUS OF IRONIC SPIRITS [aerial music]
A wife of the body, a wife of the mind,

A wife somewhat frowsy, a wife too refined:
Could the twain but grow one, and no other dames be,
No husband in Europe more steadfast than he!

SPIRIT OF THE YEARS
Cease fooling on weak waifs who love and wed
But as the unweeting Urger may bestead!—
See them withinside, douce and diamonded.

[The walls of Carlton House open, and the spectator finds himself confronting the revel.]

SCENE VII

THE SAME. THE INTERIOR OF CARLTON HOUSE

[A central hall is disclosed, radiant with constellations of candles, lamps, and lanterns, and decorated with flowering shrubs. An opening on the left reveals the Grand Council-chamber prepared for dancing, the floor being chalked with arabesques having in the centre "G. III. R.," with a crown, arms, and supporters. Orange-trees and rose-bushes in bloom stand against the walls. On the right hand extends a glittering vista of the supper-rooms and tables, now crowded with guests. This display reaches as far as the conservatory westward, and branches into long tents on the lawn.

On a dais at the chief table, laid with gold and silver plate, the Prince Regent sits like a lay figure, in a state chair of crimson and gold, with six servants at his back. He swelters in a gorgeous uniform of scarlet and gold lace which represents him as Field Marshal, and he is surrounded by a hundred-and-forty of his particular friends.

Down the middle of this state-table runs a purling brook crossed by quaint bridges, in which gold and silver fish frisk about between banks of moss and flowers. The whole scene is lit with wax candles in chandeliers, and in countless candelabra on the tables.

The people at the upper tables include the Duchess of York, looking tired from having just received as hostess most of the ladies present, except those who have come informally, Louis XVIII. of France, the Duchess of Angouleme, all the English Royal Dukes, nearly all the ordinary Dukes and Duchesses; also the Lord Chancellor of the Exchequer and other Ministers, the Lord Mayor and Lady Mayoress, all the more fashionable of the other Peers, Peeresses, and Members of Parliament, Generals, Admirals, and Mayors, with their wives. The ladies of position wear, almost to the extent of a uniform, a nodding head-dress of ostrich feathers with diamonds, and gowns of white satin embroidered in gold or silver, on which, owing to the heat, dribbles of wax from the chandeliers occasionally fall.

The Guards' bands play, and attendants rush about in blue and gold lace.]

SPIRIT OF THE PITIES
The Queen, the Regent's mother, sits not here;
Wanting, too, are his sisters, I perceive;
And it is well. With the distempered King

Immured at Windsor, sore distraught or dying,
It borders nigh on indecency
In their regard, that this loud feast is kept,
A thought not strange to many, as I read,
Even of those gathered here.

SPIRIT IRONIC
My dear phantom and crony, the gloom upon their faces is due rather to their having borrowed those
diamonds at eleven per cent than to their loyalty to a suffering monarch! But let us test the feeling. I'll
spread a report.

[He calls up the SPIRIT OF RUMOUR, who scatters whispers through the assemblage.]

A GUEST [to his neighbour]
Have you heard this report—that the King is dead?

ANOTHER GUEST
It has just reached me from the other side. Can it be true?

THIRD GUEST
I think it probable. He has been very ill all week.

PRINCE REGENT
Dead? Then my fete is spoilt, by God!

SHERIDAN
Long live the King! [He holds up his glass and bows to the Regent.]

MARCHIONESS OF HERTFORD [the new favourite, to the Regent]
The news is more natural than the moment of it! It is too cruel to you that it should happen now!

PRINCE REGENT
Damn me, though; can it be true? [He provisionally throws a regal air into his countenance.]

DUCHESS OF YORK [on the Regent's left]
I hardly can believe it. This forenoon
He was reported mending.

DUCHESS OF ANGOULEME [on the Regent's right]
On this side
They are asserting that the news is false—
That Buonaparte's child, the "King of Rome,"
Is dead, and not your royal father, sire.

PRINCE REGENT
That's mighty fortunate! Had it been true,
I should have been abused by all the world—
The Queen the keenest of the chorus, too—

Though I have been postponing this pledged feast
Through days and weeks, in hopes the King would mend,
Till expectation fusted with delay.
But give a dog a bad name—or a Prince!
So, then, it is new-come King of Rome
Who has passed or ever the world has welcomed him!...
Call him a king—that pompous upstart's son—
Beside us scions of the ancient lines!

DUKE OF BEDFORD
I think that rumour untrue also, sir. I heard it as I drove up from Woburn this evening, and it was contradicted then.

PRINCE REGENT
Drove up this evening, did ye, Duke. Why did you cut it so close?

DUKE OF BEDFORD
Well, it so happened that my sheep-sheering dinner was fixed for this very day, and I couldn't put it off. So I dined with them there at one o'clock, discussed the sheep, rushed off, drove the two-and-forty miles, jumped into my clothes at my house here, and reached your Royal Highness's door in no very bad time.

PRINCE REGENT
Capital, capital. But, 'pon my soul, 'twas a close shave!

[Soon the babbling and glittering company rise from supper, and begin promenading through the rooms and tents, the REGENT setting the example, and mixing up and talking unceremoniously with his guests of every degree. He and the group round him disappear into the remoter chambers; but may concentrate in the Grecian Hall, which forms the foreground of the scene, whence a glance can be obtained into the ball-room, now filled with dancers.

The band is playing the tune of the season, "The Regency Hornpipe," which is danced as a country-dance by some thirty couples; so that by the time the top couple have danced down the figure they are quite breathless. Two young lords talk desultorily as they survey the scene.]

FIRST LORD
Are the rumours of the King of Rome's death confirmed?

SECOND LORD
No. But they are probably true. He was a feeble brat from the first. I believe they had to baptize him on the day he was born. What can one expect after such presumption—calling him the New Messiah, and God knows what all. Ours is the only country which did not write fulsome poems about him. "Wise English!" the Tsar Alexander said drily when he heard it.

FIRST LORD
Ay! The affection between that Pompey and Caesar has begun to cool. Alexander's soreness at having his sister thrown over so cavalierly is not salved yet.

SECOND LORD
There is much beside. I'd lay a guinea there will be war between Russia and France before another year has flown.

FIRST LORD
Prinny looks a little worried to-night.

SECOND LORD
Yes. The Queen don't like the fete being held, considering the King's condition. She and her friends say it should have been put off altogether. But the Princess of Wales is not troubled that way. Though she was not asked herself she went wildly off and bought her people new gowns to come in. Poor maladroit woman!....

[Another new dance of the year is started, and another long line of couples begin to foot it.]

That's a pretty thing they are doing now. What d'ye call it?

FIRST LORD
"Speed the Plough." It is just out. They are having it everywhere. The next is to be one of those foreign things in three-eight time they call Waltzes. I question if anybody is up to dancing 'em here yet.

["Speed the Plough" is danced to its conclusion, and the band strikes up "The Copenhagen Waltz."]

SPIRIT IRONIC
Now for the wives. They both were tearing hither,
Unless reflection sped them back again;
But dignity that nothing else may bend
Succumbs to woman's curiosity,
So deem them here. Messengers, call them nigh!

[The PRINCE REGENT, having gone the round of the other rooms, now appears at the ball-room door, and stands looking at the dancers. Suddenly he turns, and gazes about with a ruffled face. He sees a tall, red-faced man near him—LORD MOIRA, one of his friends.]

PRINCE REGENT
Damned hot here, Moira. Hottest of all for me!

MOIRA
Yes, it is warm, sir. Hence I do not dance.

PRINCE REGENT
H'm. What I meant was of another order;
I spoke figuratively.

MOIRA
O indeed, sir?

PRINCE REGENT

She's here. I heard her voice. I'll swear I did!

MOIRA
Who, sir?

PRINCE REGENT
Why, the Princess of Wales. Do you think I could mistake those beastly German Ps and Bs of hers?—She asked to come, and was denied; but she's got here, I'll wager ye, through the chair-door in Warwick Street, which I arranged for a few ladies whom I wished to come privately. [He looks about again, and moves till he is by a door which affords a peep up the grand staircase.] By God, Moira, I see TWO figures up there who shouldn't be here—leaning over the balustrade of the gallery!

MOIRA
Two figures, sir. Whose are they?

PRINCE REGENT
She is one. The Fitzherbert in t'other! O I am almost sure it is! I would have welcomed her, but she bridled and said she wouldn't sit down at my table as a plain "Mrs." to please anybody. As I had sworn that on this occasion people should sit strictly according to their rank, I wouldn't give way. Why the devil did she come like this? 'Pon my soul, these women will be the death o' me!

MOIRA [looking cautiously up the stairs]
I can see nothing of her, sir, nor of the Princess either. There is a crowd of idlers up there leaning over the bannisters, and you may have mistaken some others for them.

PRINCE REGENT
O no. They have drawn back their heads. There have been such damned mistakes made in sending out the cards that the biggest w— in London might be here. She's watching Lady Hertford, that's what she's doing. For all their indifference, both of them are as jealous as two cats over the tom.

[Somebody whispers that a lady has fainted up-stairs.]

That's Maria, I'll swear! She's always doing it. Whenever I hear of some lady fainting about upon the furniture at my presence, and sending for a glass of water, I say to myself, There's Maria at it again, by God!

SPIRIT IRONIC
Now let him hear their voices once again.

[The REGENT starts as he seems to hear from the stairs the tongues of the two ladies growing louder and nearer, the PRINCESS pouring reproaches into one ear, and MRS. FITZHERBERT into the other.]

PRINCE REGENT
'Od seize 'em, Moira; this will drive me mad!
If men of blood must mate with only one
Of those dear damned deluders called the Sex,
Why has Heaven teased us with the taste for change?—
God, I begin to loathe the whole curst show!

How hot it is! Get me a glass of brandy,
Or I shall swoon off too. Now let's go out,
And find some fresher air upon the lawn.

[Exit the PRINCE REGENT, with LORDS MOIRA and YARMOUTH. The band strikes up "La Belle Catarina"
and a new figure is formed.]

SPIRIT OF THE YEARS
Phantoms, ye strain your powers unduly here,
Making faint fancies as they were indeed
The Mighty Will's firm work.

SPIRIT IRONIC
Nay, Father, nay;
The wives prepared to hasten hitherward
Under the names of some gone down to death,
Who yet were bidden. Must they not by here?

SPIRIT OF THE YEARS
There lie long leagues between a woman's word—
"She will, indeed she will!"—and acting on't.
Whether those came or no, thy antics cease,
And let the revel wear it out in peace.

[Enter SPENCER PERCEVAL the Prime Minister, a small, pale, grave-looking man, and an Under-Secretary
of State, meeting.]

UNDER-SECRETARY
Is the King of Rome really dead, and the gorgeous gold cradle wasted?

PERCEVAL
O no, he is alive and waxing strong:
That tale has been set travelling more than once.
But touching it, booms echo to our ear
Of graver import, unimpeachable.

UNDER-SECRETARY
Your speech is dark.

PERCEVAL
Well, a new war in Europe.
Before the year is out there may arise
A red campaign outscaling any seen.
Russia and France the parties to the strife—
Ay, to the death!

UNDER-SECRETARY
By Heaven, sir, do you say so?

[Enter CASTLEREAGH, a tall, handsome man with a Roman nose, who, seeing them, approaches.]

PERCEVAL
Ha, Castlereagh. Till now I have missed you here.
This news is startling for us all, I say!

CASTLEREAGH
My mind is blank on it! Since I left office
I know no more what villainy's afoot,
Or virtue either, than an anchoret
Who mortifies the flesh in some lone cave.

PERCEVAL
Well, happily that may not last for long.
But this grave pother that's just now agog
May reach such radius in its consequence
As to outspan our lives! Yes, Bonaparte
And Alexander—late such bosom-friends—
Are closing to a mutual murder-bout
At which the lips of Europe will wax wan.
Bonaparte says the fault is not with him,
And so says Alexander. But we know
The Austrian knot began their severance,
And that the Polish question largens it.
Nothing but time is needed for the clash.
And if so be that Wellington but keep
His foot in the Peninsula awhile,
Between the pestle and the mortar-stone
Of Russia and of Spain, Napoleon's brayed.
SPIRIT OF RUMOUR [to the Spirit of the Years]

Permit me now to join them and confirm,
By what I bring from far, their forecasting?

SPIRIT OF THE YEARS
I'll go. Thou knowest not greatly more than they.

[The SPIRIT OF THE YEARS enters the apartment in the shape of a pale, hollow-eye gentleman wearing an embroidered suit. At the same time re-enter the REGENT, LORDS MOIRA, YARMOUTH, KEITH, LADY HERTFORD, SHERIDAN, the DUKE OF BEDFORD, with many more notables. The band changes into the popular dance, "Down with the French," and the characters aforesaid look on at the dancers.]

SPIRIT OF THE YEARS [to Perceval]
Yes, sir; your text is true. In closest touch
With European courts and cabinets,
The imminence of dire and deadly war
Betwixt these east and western emperies

Is lipped by special pathways to mine ear.
You may not see the impact: ere it come
The tomb-worm may caress thee [Perceval shrinks]; but believe
Before five more have joined the shotten years
Whose useless films infest the foggy Past,
Traced thick with teachings glimpsed unheedingly,
The rawest Dynast of the group concerned
Will, for the good or ill of mute mankind,
Down-topple to the dust like soldier Saul,
And Europe's mouldy-minded oligarchs
Be propped anew; while garments roll in blood
To confused noise, with burning, and fuel of fire.
Nations shall lose their noblest in the strife,
And tremble at the tidings of an hour!

[He passes into the crowd and vanishes.]

PRINCE REGENT [who has heard with parted lips]
Who the devil is he?

PERCEVAL
One in the suite of the French princes, perhaps, sir?—though his tone was not monarchical. He seems
to be a foreigner.

CASTLEREAGH
His manner was that of an old prophet, and his features had a Jewish cast, which accounted for his
Hebraic style.

PRINCE REGENT
He could not have known me, to speak so freely in my presence!

SHERIDAN
I expected to see him write on the wall, like the gentleman with the Hand at Belshazzar's Feast.

PRINCE REGENT [recovering]
He seemed to know a damn sight more about what's going on in Europe, sir [to Perceval], than your
Government does, with all its secret information.

PERCEVAL
He is recently over, I conjecture, your royal Highness, and brings the latest impressions.

PRINCE REGENT
By Gad, sir, I shall have a comfortable time of it in my regency, or reign, if what he foresees be true! But
I was born for war; it is my destiny!

[He draws himself up inside his uniform and stalks away. The group dissolves, the band continuing
stridently, "Down with the French," as dawn glimmers in. Soon the REGENT'S guests begin severally and
in groups to take leave.]

SPIRIT OF THE PITIES
Behold To-morrow riddles the curtains through,
And labouring life without shoulders its cross anew!

CHORUS OF THE YEARS [aerial music]
Why watch we here? Look all around
Where Europe spreads her crinkled ground,
From Osmanlee to Hekla's mound,
Look all around!

Hark at the cloud-combed Ural pines;
See how each, wailful-wise, inclines;
Mark the mist's labyrinthine lines;

Behold the tumbling Biscay Bay;
The Midland main in silent sway;
As urged to move them, so move they.

No less through regal puppet-shows
The rapt Determinator throes,
That neither good nor evil knows!

SPIRIT OF THE PITIES
Yet I may wake and understand
Ere Earth unshape, know all things, and
With knowledge use a painless hand,
A painless hand!

[Solitude reigns in the chambers, and the scene shuts up.]

FOOTNOTES

(1) - It has been conjectured of late that these adventurous spirits were Sir Robert Wilson and, possibly, Lord Hutchinson, present there at imminent risks of their lives.

(2) - The traditional present of the rose was probably on this occasion, though it is not quite matter of certainty.

(3) - At this date.

(4) - So Madame Metternich to her husband in reporting this interview. But who shall say!

(5) - The writer has been unable to discover what became of this unhappy lady and her orphaned infants.—[Footnote The foregoing note, which appeared in the first edition of this drama, was the

means of bringing from a descendant of the lady referred to the information she remarried, and lived and died at Venice; and that both her children grew up and did well.—1909

(6) - Thomas Young of Sturminster-Newton; served twenty-one years in the Fifteenth [Footnote King's: Hussars; died 1853; fought at Vitoria, and Waterloo.

Thomas Hardy OM was an English novelist, whose Victorian realism was inspired by the Romantic movement, particularly Wordsworth, and by Dickens, who was also critical of much of Victorian society. Unlike Dickens, though, who writes primarily about cities and towns, Hardy sets much of his work in the semi-fictional country of Wessex, focusing on the decline of rural practice in England. He was known first for his novels, but towards the end of his life his poetry began to see publication and he is now considered one of the major poets of English literature, influencing various poets in the 1950-60s, most notably Philip Larkin.

Hardy was born in the hamlet of Upper Bockhampton in the Stinsford parish about three miles east of Dorchester in Dorset, England, on 2nd June 1840, in a two-storey brick and thatch cottage. His father Thomas worked as a self-employed master mason and local builder contractor, while also playing the violin. His mother, Jemima, a former maid-servant and cook, was well-read in Latin and French romances in English translation, and she enjoyed retelling the folk stories and legends of the region while she educated her son until the age of eight when he first attended the local National School in Lower Bockhampton, which had opened that year in 1848. The school was run by the National Society for Promoting the Education of the Poor in the Principles of the Established Church. From his parents, he received all of the interests and passions which would shape his writing and his life; the interest in architecture and love of music from his father, and his interest in rural lifestyles and traditions from his mother, along with a passion for literature. The Hardy family were descended from the Le Hardy family, who had resided on the Isle of Jersey since the 15th century. They had several ancestors of significant import, though at the turn of the eighteenth century the family had experienced a sharp economic collapse, a circumstance which would become key to the narrative of Tess of the d'Urbervilles. Maul Turner writes of Hardy's childhood that "apart from parental influences, Hardy's childhood was dominated by two things: the local church, and the natural world around him".

After two years at the National School, his mother enrolled him at a non-conformist school in Dorchester, run by the British and Foreign School Society, and while there he learnt Latin and French, amongst other subjects. To compliment his education, he read Greek and Roman classics in translation, and the Bible, which he knew in close detail, and he expressed a fondness for romances. In addition to his favourite authors, William Harrison Ainsworth, Walter Scott and Alexandre Dumas, he read Shakespeare's tragedies and, although ultimately he rather enjoyed school, he preferred to read books in relative solitude. While he was in Dorset, he bore witness to the decline of the traditions of the pastoral society in the face of the rise of industrialism.

Deemed unlikely by his parents and his teachers to lead a successful scholarly or clerical career, Hardy gained an apprenticeship in 1856 at the age of sixteen to John Hicks, a local architect whose speciality was in church restoration. The occupation saw him travelling extensively around Dorset, while back at the office he met another apprentice, Henry Bastow, with a similar interest in classical literature, poetry and religious matters. His only opportunity to read was in the morning before work between the hours of five and eight, and while he was working and reading here he met the poet William Barnes, also a local schoolmaster, who published poetry focusing on rural life in local dialects, and it is quite possible that it was this encounter which encouraged him to write poetry about similar themes. Within this poetry are various ideas which he picked up while on his apprenticeship, and he showed his poetry to Horace Moule, son of the vicar and a student at Queen's College, Cambridge, who, eight years Hardy's senior, became his best friend and mentor and encouraged him in his reading of Greek tragedy and more contemporary English literature. The most significant works of literature published at this time, which will no doubt have influenced Hardy, were Alfred Tennyson's poems Idylls of the King, George Meredith's Richard Feverel and Evan Harrington, Wilkie Collins's The Woman in White and George Eliot's The Mill on the Floss. Alongside these works of fiction was Charles Darwin's The Origin of Species, which had a profound influence on Hardy.

Suspending his architectural apprenticeship and heading for London in April 1862, he rented lodgings at 3, Clarence Place at Kilburn, near the Edgware Road. This move is widely considered to be the result of an unsuccessful love affair; he had already had infatuations with two girls in Dorset, who "scorned him as too young", and just prior to his move he had proposed to and been rejected by a Dorchester girl, Mary Waight, also significantly his senior. These rejections arguably encouraged him to move and begin afresh in new surroundings. While in London, he spent five years working as Arthur Blomfield's assistant architect, a noted restorer and designer of churches. Blomfield valued Hardy's work for him and put his name forward to be a member of the Architectural Association.

Meanwhile, he attended Charles Dickens's public lecture and spent time exploring the scientific and cultural offerings of London society, visiting museums and galleries, and seeing plays and operas. Further reading included the word of Herbert Spencer, Thomas Henry Huxley, John Stuart Mill, John Ruskin and Charles Darwin. The combined effect of these writers was to cause him to abandon plans of ordination in the Anglican Church, becoming increasingly disillusioned with the more institutional forms of Christianity. His own poetry flourished, spurred on by reading Robert Browning and Algernon Charles Swinburne, though it was still rejected for publication. He wrote the satire How I Built Myself a House in 1865, published in Chambers Journal and which was the first of his work to achieve recognition, winning him a prize. He also persevered with his poetry, though it remained unpublished.

By 1867 Hardy had grown tired of London and returned to Bockhampton to resume his work with John Hicks. He embarked on a love affair with his cousin, Tryphena, who lived nearby and, though there is little historical evidence of their relationship, had a profound effect on his writing at the time and appears in various guises throughout the poetry he wrote then, while also in the more obviously dedicated poem 'Thoughts of Phena'. He now began his first novel, The Poor Man and the Lady, which he submitted to Alexander Macmillan, a publishing house. Though Macmillan himself chose not to publish it, he encouraged Hardy to continue writing, and Hardy was advised to concentrate on his plotting. John Hicks's death in 1869 caused Hardy to move to Weymouth seeking employment, and at the same time he began Desperate Remedies, also refused by Macmillan but later published anonymously in three volumes by WIlliam Tinsley, in 1871. This publication saw him resolve to dedicate himself fully to his writing, though he was not yet in a position to achieve financial security or literary success. His second published novel, Under the Greenwood Tree, appeared in 1872 and its favourable reception encouraged the publication of A Pair of Blue Eyes in 1873, the most autobiographical of his novels. Next came Far From the Madding Crowd in 1874, bringing with it critical acclaim, the attention of the public and ultimately financial success. 1878 saw more success with The Return of the Native, and the ensuing years saw him rise to ever greater popularity. By now he had developed the fictional Wessex and resolved to set all of his novels there.

It was while he was working on the restoration of a church in St. Juliot, Cornwall, that he met Emma Lavinia Gifford, the local rector's sister-in-law. Captivated by her looks and her admiration for him, he fell in love with her and she would encourage his prose and poetry writing, attracted by his literary capabilities. It took them four years to marry, though, on 17th September 1874 in St Peters Church, Paddington, London. They were both thirty at marriage, though he thought she looked younger and she thought he looked older. None of Hardy's family attended the service. In 1885 the couple settled near Dorchester at Max Gate, a large mid-Victorian villa, designed by Hardy and where he spent the rest of his life. He felt very comfortable there, calling it his country retreat. The Mayor of Casterbridge was published in 1886, and its fictional setting bears many similarities to Dorchester, the market town which he knew so well. He and Emma journeyed to Italy in 1887, returning via Paris and London.

Tess of the d'Urbervilles was published in 1891 to the shock of the prudish Victorian audience who were dismayed by with the cruel presentation of a young girl's seduction and ruination by a rakish aristocrat. It only saw publication after Hardy made extensive alterations to its plot, editing or deleting vast passages. His last novel, Jude the Obscure, suffered the same levels of public outcry when it was published in 1895, and the uproar over these two novels so disturbed him that he returned to poetry, regarded by him and his audience as a purer form of artistic expression. He had not been able to make enough money as a young man to live off his poetry, but now as an adult living off the success of his novels he was able to survive comfortably, and even had a collection of his earlier poems published under the title Wessex Poems, in 1898. Meanwhile, in 1896 Emma had introduced him to the fashionable new pastime of cycling and he bought a high-quality Rover Cobb bicycle, frequently touring the Dorset countryside with his wife. They travelled extensively, to Paris, the Continent and throughout England, along with a visit to Belgium.

Hardy spent the years between 1903 and 1908 writing The Dynasts, and epic poem in blank verse about the Napoleonic Wars, and his literary authority saw him honoured by the University of Aberdeen with an honourary degree in 1905, bringing with it recognition as one of the most outstanding British authors. George V conferred on him the Order of Merit in 1910 and he was awarded the gold medal of the Royal Society of Literature in 1912. Further to his honourary degree at Aberdeen, Cambridge University named him a Doctor of Letters, his popularity continuing to grow the entire time. WIth this popularity came the dramatisation and performance of various works, and in 1914 the adaptation of The Dynasts was performed at Kingsway Theatre in London. He now proceeded to sell or donate the majority of his manuscripts, either to museums or collectors.

Emma died suddenly on 27th November 1912, and despite having grown increasingly estranged he was greatly affected by her passing, reproaching himself after her burial for not having realised the extent of her illness. He proceeded to write numerous poems expressing nostalgia for their happier times in youth, and after her death he was now taken care of by his niece and a young woman, Florence Dagdale. She was shy and charming with literary aspirations of her own, having published a few books for children, and again her admiration for him led to his infatuation with her. They married on 6th February 1914, though the wedding quickly deteriorated with it became apparent that Hardy preferred "spending much of each day closeted in his study". By now, he was in his seventies, though in spite of his ages he campaigned in favour of British involvement in the First World War. Many great writers visited him at Max Gate, for he left less and less.

In 1924 hew witnessed a stage production of Tess of the d'Urbervilles, a performance so powerful that Hardy promptly became infatuated with the young actress playing Tess. From 1920 to 1927 he worked, in secret, on his autobiography, which was published in two volumes in 1928 and 1930 as the work of Florence Hardy. She made various emendations to the text, having typed the manuscripts, probably reducing the references to Emma and adding anecdotes and referring to letters. His 87th birthday passed, and he seemed increasingly weaker, staying in bed for long periods, until in 1927 he fell gravely ill, dying on the 11th January 1928. Just prior to his death, he asked Florence to read a verse from The Rubaiyat of Omar Khayyam,

Oh, Thou, who Man of baser Earth didst make,
And ev'n with Paradise devise the snake:
For all the Sin wherewith the Face of Man
Is blackened - Man's forgiveness give - and take!

His body was cremated and the ashes interred in Poet's Corner in the South Transept in Westminster Abbey. The official of the two funerals was attended by the then Prime Minister Stanley Baldwin, leader of the Opposition Ramsay MacDonald, the heads of Oxford and Cambridge University colleges where Hardy had been honoured, and various significant literary figures such as James Barrie, George Bernard Shaw and Rudyard Kipling. Meanwhile, his heart was buried alongside his first wife in Stinsford churchyard, Dorchester. He is best remembered by Evelyn Hardy, the critic, who writes "Hardy's life was not primarily one of action. He was by nature a scholar and a writer: it is what goes on in the mind that holds us, and Hardy's was rich with stored impressions".

THOMAS HARDY – A CONCISE BIBLIOGRAPHY

Prose

Hardy divided his novels and collected short stories into three types

Novels of Character and Environment

The Poor Man and the Lady (1867, unpublished and now lost)
Under the Greenwood Tree: A Rural Painting of the Dutch School (1872)
Far from the Madding Crowd (1874)
The Return of the Native (1878)
The Mayor of Casterbridge: The Life and Death of a Man of Character (1886)
The Woodlanders (1887)
Wessex Tales (1888, a collection of short stories)
Tess of the d'Urbervilles: A Pure Woman Faithfully Presented (1891)
Life's Little Ironies (1894, a collection of short stories)
Jude the Obscure (1895)

Romances and Fantasies

A Pair of Blue Eyes: A Novel (1873)
The Trumpet-Major (1880)
Two on a Tower: A Romance (1882)
A Group of Noble Dames (1891, a collection of short stories)
The Well-Beloved: A Sketch of a Temperament (1897) (first published as a serial from 1892)

Novels of Ingenuity

Desperate Remedies: A Novel (1871)
The Hand of Ethelberta: A Comedy in Chapters (1876)
A Laodicean: A Story of To-day (1881)

Short Stories

How I Built Myself A House (1865)
Destiny and a Blue Cloak (1874)
The Thieves Who Couldn't Stop Sneezing (1877)
The Duchess of Hamptonshire (1878)
The Distracted Preacher (1879)
Fellow-Townsmen (1880)
The Honourable Laura (1881)
What The Shepherd Saw (1881)
A Tradition of Eighteen Hundred and Four (1882)
The Three Strangers (1883)
The Romantic Adventures of a Milkmaid (1883)
Interlopers at the Knap (1884)
A Mere Interlude (1885)
A Tryst at an Ancient Earthwork (1885)
Alicia's Diary (1887)
The Waiting Supper (1887–88)
The Withered Arm (1888)

A Tragedy of Two Ambitions (1888)
The First Countess of Wessex (1889)
Anna, Lady Baxby (1890)
The Lady Icenway (1890)
Lady Mottisfont (1890)
The Lady Penelope (1890)
The Marchioness of Stonehenge (1890)
Squire Petrick's Lady (1890)
Barbara of the House of Grebe (1890)
The Melancholy Hussar of The German Legion (1890)
Absent-Mindedness in a Parish Choir (1891)
The Winters and the Palmleys (1891)
For Conscience' Sake (1891)
Incident in Mr. Crookhill's Life (1891)
The Doctor's Legend (1891)
Andrey Satchel and the Parson and Clerk (1891)
The History of the Hardcomes (1891)
Netty Sargent's Copyhold (1891)
On The Western Circuit (1891)
A Few Crusted Characters: Introduction (1891)
The Superstitious Man's Story (1891)
Tony Kytes, the Arch-Deceiver (1891)
To Please His Wife (1891)
The Son's Veto (1891)
Old Andrey's Experience as a Musician (1891)
Our Exploits At West Poley (1892–93)
Master John Horseleigh, Knight (1893)
The Fiddler of the Reels (1893)
An Imaginative Woman (1894)
The Spectre of the Real (1894)
A Committee-Man of 'The Terror' (1896)
The Duke's Reappearance (1896)
The Grave by the Handpost (1897)
A Changed Man (1900)
Enter a Dragoon (1900)
Blue Jimmy: The Horse Stealer (1911)
Old Mrs. Chundle (1929)
The Unconquerable (1992)

Poetry Collections
Wessex Poems and Other Verses (1898)
Poems of the Past and the Present (1901)

Time's Laughingstocks and Other Verses (1909)
Satires of Circumstance (1914)
Moments of Vision (1917)
Collected Poems (1919)
Late Lyrics and Earlier with Many Other Verses (1923)
Human Shows, Far Phantasies, Songs and Trifles (1925)
Winter Words in Various Moods and Metres (1928)

Drama

The Dynasts: An Epic-Drama of the War with Napoleon (verse drama)
The Dynasts, Part 1 (1904)
The Dynasts, Part 2 (1906)
The Dynasts, Part 3 (1908)
The Famous Tragedy of the Queen of Cornwall at Tintagel in Lyonnesse (1923) (one-act play)

www.ingramcontent.com/pod-product-compliance
Lightning Source LLC
Chambersburg PA
CBHW070104070426
42448CB00038B/1603